The New Constitution Movement

**A Blueprint for Constitutional Reform
for St. Lucia, the OECS and the Caribbean**

*Advocating a No-Party Government
in a Multi-Party State*

By
Martinus François

Order this book online at www.trafford.com
or email orders@trafford.com

Most Trafford titles are also available at major online book retailers.

Print information available on the last page.

ISBN: 978-1-4669-1388-2 (sc)
ISBN: 978-1-4669-1389-9 (e)

Trafford rev. 01/19/2018

 www.trafford.com

North America & international
toll-free: 1 888 232 4444 (USA & Canada)
fax: 812 355 4082

Contents

DEDICATION

This book is dedicated to the memory of the late Madame Justice Suzie d' Auvergne (Retired), chairperson of the now disbanded Constitutional Review Commission (under Statutory Instrument No. 50 of 2004), who passed away on August 18, 2014.

Preface

One cannot discuss the role and intendment of the political party in St. Lucia, the OECS and the Caribbean, as this book sets out to do, without considering the thoughts of the eminent Trinidadian intellectual, the late C.L.R. James.

The Life and Voyages of Christopher Columbus
Boston: Twayne Publishers, 1981, p. 165
WASHINGTON IRVING

A shallow courtier present, impatient of the honours paid to Columbus, and meanly jealous of him as a foreigner, abruptly asked him whether he thought that, in case he had not discovered the Indias, there were not other men in Spain, who would have been capable of the enterprise? To this Columbus made no immediate reply, but, taking an egg, invited the company to make it stand on one end. Everyone attempted it, but in vain; whereupon he struck it upon the table so as to break the end, and left it standing on the broken part; illustrating in this simple manner, that when he had once shown the way to the new world, nothing was easier than to follow it.

A few years before his death in 1988, someone asked him: *"If a group of Trinidadians came up to you and said '...we're worried about the condition of Trinidad & Tobago and we have decided to form a political party', what kind of advice would you give them?"*

The sage replied: *"I would ask them, number one, have you worked out a basic philosophy of politics which you are going to put into action?"*

We are now living in the 21ˢᵗ century; facing all its challenges at a time when there is widespread interest in, and dire need for, new initiatives and fresh approaches to the promotion of economic and social development in St. Lucia, the OECS, and by extension, the Caribbean. But our social scientists and thinkers seem to have reached an inevitable crossroads. Since supposed decolonization, there has been a search on to find a path of development that would be endemically applicable to this region and guide its quest for development and free us once and for all from the shackles of slavery and dependency.

However, after all this time, the region's economies/ societies are still heavily dependent on foreign variables mainly because of paths to development which have been followed that are demonstrably irrelevant to the region.

This has produced a condition such as Errol Barrow in 1982 described as *"the mendicant dependency syndrome: We do not have any pride anymore because we are joining the ranks of the beggars. We have developed a mendicant mentality, and we are even boasting now of our mendicancy, our success in begging."*

The embarrassing fussing and fighting by the Cabinet/ Government of St. Lucia over China and Taiwan in 2007 is a case in point.

Addressing the Caribbean Community Heads of Government Conference in Georgetown, Guyana, on July 3, 1986, the late Prime Minister of Barbados, Errol Barrow, said: *"The University of the West Indies has provided us over more than one generation with some very remarkable social scientists. I recall with a certain pride the excellent work which was done by the New World Group over the 1960s. Every major sector of our economic life has come under their scrutiny: Sugar, Bauxite, Oil, Tourism. Girvan and Thomas and Carrington and Brewster and Beckford, and, of course, Lloyd Best. Investigation which has always concerned the Institute of Social and Economic Research. They proved beyond any doubt that this region is not lacking in intellectual human resources. But in spite of all this excellent work, an important link was missing. All this analysis, all this valuable organization of information never got very far beyond the small circle of specialists for and by whom it was written. There was no link between that great storehouse of knowledge and the toiling*

*mass of workers who are the motor force of any society. The
analysis may be brilliant, the recommendations very ingenious;
but these will serve a very limited purpose if their content
does not become an essential part of the consciousness of the
working population."*

One leading Caribbean political mind, the late Tim Hector
of Antigua & Barbuda, commenting on the massive defeat of
the Erskine Sandiford Government of Barbados in 1994 under
the burden of "structural adjustment", opined that the advent
of structural adjustment in the Caribbean represented not only
a failure of the Caribbean's political community but that of the
intellectual community as well.

The failure of political management in St. Lucia, the OECS
and the wider Caribbean over the past sixty-seven (67) years
marks an enormous setback which has still not been fully
recognized: it is a defeat of historic proportions; it represents
the abandonment of ambition; acquiescence in decline; and
a throwing-in-of-the-towel acceptance that nothing else is
possible.

Our recent political history in the Caribbean shows that
structural adjustment, accompanied by all its warts and
indignity of foreign supervision, had always been an accident
waiting to happen: over six (6) decades on since adult suffrage
in 1951, our social, political, economic, cultural, intellectual,
jurisprudential, administrative, institutional and constitutional
forms have, for the most part, been imitated rather than created,
borrowed rather than relevant.

The effect of history on our lives in the Caribbean has
been, sadly, psychological. They brought us here during the
Middle Passage and later came as conquistadores with gun in
one hand and bible in the other as they took away our lands.

However inscrutable the economic problems facing the
region, we are viable, functioning societies with the strength
of intellect and generosity of inventiveness to understand and
grapple with our development problems in a spirit of self-reliance.

How else could a small island like St. Lucia produce not
one (1) but two (2) Nobel Laureates in Sir Arthur Lewis and
Derek Walcott in one (1) generation while many vast nations
and civilizations never produced one (1)? St. Lucia has the
highest Nobel Laureate ratio *per capita* in the world.

We must now see ourselves as the new conquistadores;
conquistadores, though, not to conquer and destroy but to
renew and rebuild. In the words of Derek Walcott: *"There are
no worlds to conquer but worlds to rebuild."*

Introduction

I t is becoming increasingly obvious that traditional democracy is being stridently shaken across the globe. The collapse of authoritarian regimes in Eastern Europe, Africa, the Middle East, even Western Europe (Brexit) means that popular movements for reform and decentralization are attracting favourable attention the world over.

Whatever else is happening across the globe, for us in the postcolonial Caribbean, the way power continues to dominate increasing aspects of our lives holds poignant significance— not least because we have only relatively recently crawled out of an exceedingly oppressive past.

That process has rendered our colonially inherited and ossified, quasi-democratic system out-of-date and informed a new dynamic social, political and economic movement seeking to win for ordinary people some effective control over their own life chances.

It is self-evident that neocolonial government and politics in St. Lucia, the OECS and the Caribbean still exists in a pyramid-like structure of society; with the oblivious "unknowing" masses at the bottom and their "all knowing" leaders at the top; as opposed to the egg-shaped society in which we actually live in the 21st century, influenced by the information revolution; where the majority of the people in the middle numerically predominate and should define the dominant ethos of society.

Our colonially inherited hierarchical, top-down, bureaucratic organization was designed for the period of colonization when mass standardized services were sufficient and those at the top were in command of all information and knowledge. We're in the 21st century now; in a world that has become a global village.

Higher public expectations, choice, and the information revolution have rendered this form of organization simply too cumbersome, inefficient, expensive, and an anachronism.

The case against the neocolonial, Westminster model of St. Lucian, OECS and Caribbean politics is not that it is quasi-democratic or out of synch with the 21st century—though it is both of these things—or even that its lack of accountability, transparency and responsibility renders it easily amenable to abuse.

It is that the values it embodies and transmits are pre-democratic; that it reflects and sustains a political culture of subservience at every level of society that is becoming increasingly obsolete, restrictive and offensive; that it symbolizes small nations/states populated by subjects, not citizens; and that its vision of society is one in which the rulers rule and the ruled know their place.

Moreover, its values and assumptions are too hierarchical and the powers it exercises are the rulers'; not the people's. Often in St. Lucia, the OECS and the wider Caribbean this has resulted in cases of blatant and malicious abuse of power and militated against the growth of a truly civic culture of true democracy.

The basic philosophy of **THE NEW CONSTITUTION MOVEMENT** is that, hierarchical, centralized bureaucracies designed in the mid-20th century simply do not work for us effectively in the rapidly changing, information-rich, knowledge-intensive society and economy of the 21st century. Therefore, St. Lucian, OECS, and by extension, Caribbean Government has to be *reinvented* for a 21st century society; that the outdated and anachronistic politics of St. Lucia, the OECS and the Caribbean is in dire need of a new dynamic initiative for democratic reform.

The challenge for St. Lucian, OECS and Caribbean democracy is to open up greater opportunities for the participation of the youth and others in society who have acquired new skills, expertise, knowledge and experience.

The fact is, building a new twenty-first-century-looking society on the wreckage of the old colonial and quasi-colonial structures involves the design of new, more appropriate political systems in St. Lucia, the OECS and the entire Caribbean which must be altogether tougher, more challenging, more positive, more ambitious, more inspirational, more generational and, above all, more transformational.

Clearly, the stakes are high but the risk of not overhauling our political institutions are even greater and the sooner we begin the better because the prize is great.

We will need to radically overhaul or even scrap many of our hitherto sacred cows of the colonially inherited Westminster system to the point that they may even lose some of their traditional meanings: the Monarchy, the Office of Governor-General, the Executive Branch, the Office of Prime Minister, the Cabinet System, the Legislative Branch, the Senate, the Office of Leader of the Opposition, the Political Parties, the Public Service, Local and Municipal Government, and last but not least, Regional Integration.

CHAPTER 1

The Past as Prologue to The Future

The Voice of the People is the Voice of God
JEAN JACQUES ROUSSEAU

Before the full evolution of political democracy as we know it today many nations of the Western World (including Great Britain, France, Germany, Switzerland, the Netherlands, Belgium and Italy) had adopted some form of democratic rule. However, what most of these countries were interested in was governmental or political democracy (a kind of majoritarianism) characterized by a Parliament, a limited right to vote, and the Cabinet system. It was not until the late 18th to early 19th centuries that there was much concern with SOCIAL or economic DEMOCRACY. There was the perennial fear that this might constitute a serious threat to the position of the hereditary aristocracy, or force the tycoons of industry and commerce to disgorge large chunks of their wealth for the benefit of the social majority, the poor and underprivileged.

But in order to understand the true meaning of democracy, we need to consider its historical origins. **Jean Jacques Rousseau** is credited to be the founder of the political ideal we know as democracy. The most significant of his writings on political theory was **The Social Contract** (1762) where he upheld the popular thesis that men had originally lived in a state of nature where no-one had to sue or complain to maintain his rights against others as obtains today. Indeed there were very few charges of conflict of any sort because private property simply did not exist and every man was the equal of his neighbour.

Eventually, however, evils arose; primarily because of selfishness, greed and the cupidity of man. Some men staked off plots of land and said: "This is mine." Rousseau believed it was this type of attitude that brought about the various degrees of inequality and "cheating trickery", "insolent pomp" and "insatiable ambition" soon came to dominate the relations among men.

The only hope of security was now for men to establish a CIVIL SOCIETY and to surrender all their rights to the community. This they did by means of a SOCIAL CONTRACT, in which each individual agreed with the whole body of individuals to submit to the WILL OF THE MAJORITY— bringing the concept of the State into existence.

The State, of course, should not be confused with the Government, as is popularly the case. Rousseau regarded the State as the POLITICALLY ORGANIZED COMMUNITY, which has the supreme function of expressing the general will.

The Government, on the other hand, is simply the EXECUTIVE AGENT of the State. Its function is NOT TO FORMULATE the general will but TO CARRY IT OUT.

The authority of the State (THE PEOPLE, THE MAJORITY) cannot be represented (as for example, by a parliamentary representative) BUT MUST BE EXPRESSED DIRECTLY THROUGH THE ENACTMENT OF FUNDAMENTAL LAWS BY THE PEOPLE THEMSELVES.

Moreover, the community, the people, the majority, can set the Government up and PULL IT DOWN WHENEVER IT LIKES.

The basic postulation of **The Social Contract** is that each contracting person puts his person into the community under the supreme direction of the general will. In place of the individual personality of each contracting person the social contract creates a collective body, which receives from the act of union its common identity. This newly formed public body by the union of all other persons is the *body politic*. The persons concerned collectively are *the people*.

Rousseau believed that the position in which the people find themselves as a result of this social contract is preferable to that in which they might have been without it. Instead of a haphazard and precarious way of life (whereby every man is for himself and the devil takes the hindmost, or the law of the jungle) they find themselves in one that is better and more secure. Instead of their individual strength, which others might overcome, they now have a right which social union makes invincible. Instead of untrammelled natural freedom and independence, they now have *liberty*.

What a man loses by way of the social contract is natural (unlimited) liberty. What he gains is CIVIL LIBERTY. Natural liberty, therefore, is limited only by the strength of the individual whereas civil liberty is necessarily limited by the general will—the will of the majority.

In addition, for such physical inequality as nature may have set up between men, the social contract substitutes an equality that is moral and fair. By it, men who may be unequal in strength or intelligence, for example, become in every way equal by constitutional and legal right.

Further, Rousseau insisted that each individual, in becoming a party to the social contract, gave up all his rights to the community and agreed to submit collectively to the general will.

It follows that the sovereign power of the State, the majority, when Civil Society is formed, is subject to NO LIMITATION. The general will, EXPRESSED THROUGH THE VOTE OF THE MAJORITY, is veritably the Court of Final Appeal. What THE MAJORITY decides IS ALWAYS RIGHT in the political sense and it is absolutely binding UPON EVERY CITIZEN (including those who temporarily form the executive agency of the State, the Government).

Under this true democracy, it may be assumed that the minority will continue to enjoy full liberty of expression, but this may not necessarily be so. The only sovereign right of the minority is the right to strive to become the majority. As long as a particular group remains a minority, its members cannot claim any rights of individual action beyond the control of the State.

However, freedom of speech, freedom of the press and other fundamental human rights and freedoms are considered essential components of the Rousseauan democratic ideal; but none is regarded as sacrosanct and beyond the control of the majority.

To be sure, if these fundamental rights were entirely obliterated by the State, democracy would cease to exist; however, the majority has the right to limit them when there is a clear and immediate danger to the public interest.

Historically, therefore, all that Rousseauan democracy has really required is that all ideas that do not represent a threat to the interest of the majority should be tolerated and minorities should be allowed to strive to become the majority.

Historically, political democracy meant, above all, that the majority of the people should be allowed to speak for the entire nation, and that in forming that majority the votes of all the citizens should be equal. As a corollary, the machinery of the democratic State should include such facilities as adult suffrage (the right of all adults to vote), free and fair elections and adequate control by the people of the Government. And in order that this machinery should operate effectively, the citizens must have the right to form and organize political parties and to choose freely among them.

It was Rousseau's doctrine of the absolute supremacy of the majority, together with his belief in the common man that, more than anything else, gave us the ideal THE VOICE OF THE PEOPLE IS THE VOICE OF GOD.

In fact, in its original, historic meaning, DEMOCRACY is inseparable from the idea of the sovereignty of the masses. WHAT THE MAJORITY OF THE CITIZENS WILLS SHOULD BE THE SUPREME LAW OF THE LAND, FOR THE VOICE OF THE PEOPLE IS THE VOICE OF GOD.

The constitutional democracy which is now practised in the Western World and the Caribbean is, of course, not Rousseauan democracy but in fact the LIBERAL (or REPRESENTATIVE or PARLIAMENTARY) DEMOCRACY of **John Locke**. This type of democracy, LIBERALISM also called INDIVIDUALISM, asserts the absolute right of the individual to do or say or live as he pleases so long as he does not harm his neighbour.

True (or Rousseauan) democracy and liberalism have now come to be used interchangeably as if they were one and the same thing. Originally, however, they were entirely separate ideals and still are. Historic (or Rousseauan) democracy included a belief in the natural equality of all men, opposition to hereditary privilege, and an abiding faith in the wisdom and virtue of THE MASSES.

Lockean liberalism is more concerned with the defence of individual rights than with the democratic enforcement of popular rule. In his **Second Treatise of Civil Government** (1690) Locke developed the theory of limited Government that was used to justify the new system of parliamentary rule set up in England during the latter end of the 17th century. He maintained that originally all men had lived in a state of nature in which absolute freedom and equality prevailed, and there was no Government of any sort. The only law was the law of nature, which each individual enforced in order to protect his natural rights to life, liberty and property.

It was not long, however, until men started to perceive that the inconvenience of the state of nature greatly outweighed its advantages. With every individual attempting to enforce his own rights; anarchy, confusion and insecurity were the inevitable results. Accordingly, the people agreed among themselves to establish a Civil Society, to set up a Government and to surrender certain powers to it.

If the Government exceeded or abused the authority expressly granted in the political contract, it became tyrannical and the people had the right to dissolve it or rebel against it and to overthrow it. Although he proclaimed a right of Revolution, Locke was, however, no enemy of political order and authority.

Rulers had the right to rule—to use their political power for the common good. But all men had the right to resist the ruler who manifestly abused his power.

Subject to Locke's conception of Government, therefore, was the notion of trust; there exists between the people and the Government a fiduciary relationship. The people put their trust in the Government: a ruler who betrays this trust may be overthrown—he has put himself in a state of war with the people and each one of these has the same right to resist him as they would any unjust aggressor.

And John Locke was in no doubt who should be blamed for disorder and rebellion. To disturb just Government was for him a breach of natural law; to rebel without just cause was for Locke unjust: *"But when the oppressed people resist tyranny it is not they who disturb Government or bring a state of war. Rebellion is an opposition not to persons but to authority. A tyrant has no authority. It is tyrants that are the real rebels."*

Though Locke defended the supremacy of the Legislature, with the Executive primarily as the agent of the Legislative Branch; unlike Rousseau, he refused to concede to the people's deputies an unlimited power. He believed no matter how large a majority, the people's deputies cannot demand the restriction of freedom of speech or the confiscation and redistribution of private property. That if such action is taken it would be illegal and justify effective measures of resistance on the part of the majority of citizens.

Locke, of course, was more concerned with protecting individual rights than promoting *social justice*, social stability or social progress.

The influence of few political philosophers in the history of the world has exceeded that of Rousseau and Locke. Locke's doctrines of individual rights, limited Government and the right of resistance against tyranny were not only an important source of French Revolutionary theory in the eighteenth century but they also found ready acceptance in American thought as well. Not only did they furnish most of the theoretical foundation for the colonial revolt against British oppression, they were also reflected so clearly in the **American Declaration of Independence** that whole passages of that historical document might almost certainly have been copied from Locke's **Second Treatise of Civil Government**.

The French charter of liberties, the **Declaration of the Rights of Man and of the Citizen**, issued in September 1789, was largely modelled after the liberal political techniques of Locke. The French Declaration was a typical middle-class document in keeping with the first, bourgeoisie stage of the Revolution.

Property was declared to be a natural right as well as liberty, security and "resistance to oppression". No-one was to be deprived of anything he owned except in case of public necessity, and then only on condition that he should have been "previously and equitably indemnified". Proper consideration was also to be given to personal rights. Freedom of speech, religious toleration and liberty of the press were held to be inviolable.

Every citizen was declared to be entitled to equality of treatment in the courts. No-one was to be imprisoned or otherwise punished except in accordance with due process of law. Sovereignty was affirmed to reside in the people, and officers of the Government were made subject to deposition if they abused the power conferred upon them.

However, nothing was said about the right of the common man to an adequate share of the wealth he produced or even to protection by the State in case of inability to earn a living. The authors of the Declaration of Rights were bourgeois, not socialist; nor were they particularly interested in the economic welfare of the masses.

By the summer of 1792, the French Revolution had entered its second or *radical* stage. The second stage differed from the first which was dominated by the bourgeoisie. Now it was radical extremists representing the proletariat of Paris who were largely responsible for determining the nature of the movement. The liberal philosophy of Locke was replaced by the radical, egalitarian doctrines of Rousseau.

But the second stage of the French Revolution was not only radical but also violent. There were many factors to explain this spectacular transition from a comparatively moderate, middle-class phase to a stage of radicalism and turmoil. The Revolution in its beginning had held out what appeared to be glorious promises of equality and *social justice* for every citizen. Hope had been built, particularly on the **Declaration of the Rights of Man and of the Citizen**, in spite of its emphasis upon the sanctity of private property. But now after more than three years of social and political upheaval it was just as hard as it had been before for the urban worker to earn his bread.

Another disappointment came about when the common man discovered after the Constitution of 1791 that he was not even allowed to vote.

Ever more clearly the realization dawned that he had simply exchanged one set of masters for another. Given such a scenario he was bound to be attracted by the rabble-rousing preaching of radical extremists such as the Rousseauan disciple, Maximilien François Robespierre, a firebrand lawyer and politician, who offered to lead him to the Promised Land of security and plenty.

Robespierre had adopted the belief that the philosophy of Rousseau held the one great hope of salvation for all mankind. To put this philosophy into practice he was ready to employ any means that would bring results, regardless of the cost to him or to others. This passionate loyalty to a gospel that exalted the masses won him a following and he eventually became the most famous and perhaps the greatest of the radical Revolutionary leaders.

A second cause of the transition to a radical stage was the accumulated momentum of the Revolution itself. Every great movement of this kind generates an atmosphere of discontent, which is breathed more deeply by some men than by others. The result is often the emergence of a kind of professional Revolutionist who is eternally dissatisfied no matter how much has been accomplished. He denounces the leaders of the Revolution in its primary stage even more scathingly than he condemns the adherents of the old order. For him, no price of violence and chaos is too great to pay in order to purchase the fulfilment of his own ideals.

> **Shakespeare: A Critical Study of His Mind and Art (1875)**
>
> EDWARD DOWDEN
>
> *It is idealists who create political terror; they are free from all desire for blood-letting; but to them the lives of men and women are accidents; the lives of ideas are the true realities; and, armed with an abstract principle and a suspicion, they perform deeds which are at once beautiful and hideous.*

No movement which had so thoroughly shaken the foundations of society could ever have passed into history without leaving a train of momentous results. Its influence was of great benefit to mankind as a whole and reverberated through the remaining years of the 18ᵗʰ century and most of the years of the 19ᵗʰ century. It was felt in scores of nations throughout the Western World.

Other enduring achievements of the French Revolution included the fact that it dealt a powerful blow to the doctrine of absolute monarchy and the divine rights of kings, the destruction of serfdom and the feudal system, the separation of Church and State, the wider and more equitable distribution of land through the breaking down of great estates and the abolition of slavery in the French colonies.

In 1795 two thousand St. Lucian slaves, who became known as "brigands", in collaboration with French Revolutionaries, rallied to the heady slogan *"LIBERTY, EQUALITY and FRATERNITY"* and, what can be termed the first "St. Lucian Revolution", seized control of the island from the British before it was recaptured by the latter. (St. Lucia, of course, is famous for changing colonial hands fourteen (14) times between the French and the British.)

The groundwork for two of Napoleon's most significant achievements, his educational reforms and his codification of laws, was actually prepared by Revolutionary leaders.

Rousseau's dogmas of equality and the supremacy of the majority were the chief inspiration of the second and popular stage of the French Revolution. But Rousseau's influence was not confined to his own country. Some of his theories made their way to America and were echoed in certain of the principles of both Jacksonian and Jeffersonian Democracy.

From 1789 to 1801, the conservatives, the money power and the big landowners held the reigns of power in America. The Democratic-Republicans gained control as a result of the election of Thomas Jefferson to the presidency in 1800. This event is often referred to as the Jeffersonian Revolution on the premise that Jefferson was the champion of the masses and of the political power of the underprivileged. Instead of being a follower of Locke, which was hitherto the norm of the American establishment, Jefferson was a disciple of Rousseau.

Jefferson's movement had a number of cardinal objectives which conformed to democracy in its Rousseauan, historic meaning; although it led the campaign for the addition of a Bill of Rights to the federal Constitution and was almost exclusively responsible for this success.

However, although professing devotion to the principle of separation of powers between the Judicial, Executive and Legislative Branches of Government, Jefferson actually believed in the supremacy of the people's deputies and viewed with abhorrence attempts by the Executive and Judicial Branches to increase their power at the expense of the power of the people.

Thomas Jefferson was a vigorous opponent of special privilege, whether of birth or wealth. Three of his most typical ideals were (1) decentralized Government (2) periodic revisions of Constitutions and laws and (3) the importance of public education.

He also stressed the VALUE OF LOCAL GOVERNMENT TO THE EXTENT OF ADVOCATING PRIMARY <u>TOWN-MEETING ASSEMBLIES</u> FOR THE EXERCISE OF A LARGE PROPORTION OF PUBLIC POWERS.

Jefferson urged that CONSTITUTIONS AND LAWS SHOULD BE SUBMITTED TO THE PEOPLE FOR THEIR APPROVAL OR REJECTION EVERY NINETEEN OR TWENTY YEARS, ON THE PREMISE THAT NO ONE GENERATION HAS THE RIGHT TO BIND ITS SUCCESSORS IN PERPETUITY. SUNSET LEGISLATION!

In his later life Jefferson completed plans for an elaborate system of public education. There was to be free instruction for all children in the elementary schools, and scholarships were to be provided in district colleges and in state universities for a limited number of students selected on the basis of intelligence and achievement; thus ensuring opportunity for all and not simply for the well-born and the rich. The persons thus educated would be available for selection as "natural aristocrats" by enlightened citizens who had received enough knowledge to recognize good men when they saw them.

Yet another relevant and profound political thinker among the great philosophers of the 18th century was Baron François Montesquieu. In his celebrated **Spirit of Laws** (1748), Montesquieu brought new methods and new conceptions into the theory of the State. Instead of attempting to found a science of Government by pure deduction, like Locke and Rousseau, he followed the Aristotelian logic of studying actual political systems as they were supposed to have operated in the past. He tended to ignore the Lockean ideas of natural rights and the contractual origin of the State and taught that the meaning of the law of nature is to be found in the facts of history.

Montesquieu, a French lawyer and politician, denied that THERE IS ANY ONE PERFECT FORM OF GOVERNMENT SUITABLE FOR ALL PERSONS UNDER ALL CONDITIONS. He maintained, on the contrary, that POLITICAL INSTITUTIONS IN ORDER TO BE SUCCESSFUL MUST HARMONIZE WITH THE PHYSICAL CONDITION AND THE LEVEL OF SOCIAL ADVANCEMENT OF THE NATIONS THEY INTEND TO SERVE.

He therefore posited that despotism is best suited for countries of vast domain, limited monarchy to those of moderate size and republican Government to those of small extent.

For his own country, France, he opined that a limited monarchy would be the most appropriate form; since he regarded the nation as too large to be made into a republic unless on some kind of federal plan.

Montesquieu is especially famous for his theory of **the separation of powers**. He avowed that it is a natural tendency of man to abuse any extent of power entrusted to him; and that, consequently, every Government, regardless of its form, is liable to degenerate into despotism. To prevent such an outcome, he argued that the authority of the Government should be broken up into its three natural divisions: Legislative, Executive and Judicial. THAT WHENEVER ANY TWO OR MORE OF THESE BRANCHES ARE ALLOWED TO BE UNITED IN THE SAME HANDS, LIBERTY IS AT AN END.

The only effective way to avoid tyranny is to enable each branch of Government to act as a check upon the other two. He believed that the Executive should have power by means of the veto to curb the encroachment of the Law-making Branch; the Legislature, in turn, should have the authority of impeachment in order to restrain the Executive; and an independent Judiciary should be vested with power to protect individual rights against arbitrary acts of either the Legislature or the Executive.

Montesquieu was no Rousseauan democrat but a Lockean bourgeois who was more than a little afraid of the power of the masses—hence his neat little scheme to empower the Executive with a veto to curb the power of the people's deputies. This favourite device of his was certainly not intended to facilitate the growth of TRUE DEMOCRACY. In fact, its purpose was largely the opposite—to prevent the absolute supremacy of the majority, expressed as it normally would be through the people's deputies in the Legislature.

However, Montesquieu's principle of the separation of powers was nevertheless influential. It was incorporated, not surprisingly, in the bourgeoisie and first of the Governments set up under the French Revolution; and found its way with few changes into the Constitution of the United States.

The lesson of the Americans in 1776 and the French in 1789, which serves as the crucibles for the modern ideal of equality of citizenship, is that processes that flout the basic values of democratic citizenship cannot produce democratic results.

In the revered words of the **American Declaration of Independence** on July 4, 1776: "When in the course of human events it becomes necessary for one people to dissolve the political bands which have connected them with another, and to assume among the powers of the earth, the separate and equal station to which the Laws of Nature and of Nature's God entitles them, a decent respect to the opinions of mankind requires that they should declare the causes which impel them to the separation.

"We hold these truths to be self-evident, that all men are created equal. That they are endowed by their Creator with certain inalienable Rights, that among these are Life, Liberty and the pursuit of Happiness. That to secure these rights Governments are instituted among men, deriving their just powers from the consent of the governed. That whenever any form of Government becomes destructive of these ends, it is the Right of the People to alter or to abolish it, and to institute new Government, laying its foundation on such principles and organizing its powers in such form, as to them shall seem most likely to secure their Safety and Happiness.

"Prudence, indeed, will dictate that Governments long established should not be changed for light and transient causes; and accordingly all experience hath shown that mankind is more disposed to suffer while evils are sufferable, than to right themselves by abolishing the forms to which they are accustomed. But when a long train of abuses and usurpations, pursuing invariably the same object evinces a design to reduce them under absolute despotism, it is their Right, their Duty, to throw off such Government, and to provide new Guards for their future security."

CHAPTER 2

The Early 20th Century

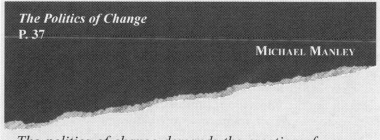

The Politics of Change
P. 37

MICHAEL MANLEY

The politics of change demands the creation of a mass political organization, which is capable of organizing mass response, mass understanding and mass involvement in the process of change.

The rebellion against imperialism or colonialism (as it is now more commonly called) was one of the least obvious but nevertheless important consequences of World War I—a war mainly in Europe and the Middle East, from July 28, 1914, to November 11, 1918; where the United States, Great Britain, France, Russia, and their allies were on one side; and Germany, Italy, Japan, and their allies were on the other.

For many centuries before the War, the European powers had succeeded in imposing their rule upon the large proportion of the teeming hordes of South-east Asia, India, the Middle East, Africa, Latin America and the Caribbean; ostensibly with a divine mission to carry the blessings of civilization to benighted natives.

In many cases, the civilizing process was merely a veneer of exploitation palliated by scraps of education, sanitation and health care. So long as the people saw little hope of changing their status they accepted the rule of the European with no more than feeble protest.

However, the spectacle of the great Christian nations killing each other on the battlefield blunted their pretence of morality. Moreover, World War I also facilitated the triumph of communism in Russia and the dissemination of its appeal to the subjects of capitalist powers to throw off their oppressors.

These developments inevitably connived to produce in colonial dependencies a spirit of revolt against colonialism; which culminated at a time when world society, which was becoming more aware of humanity's ethical and moral values, made an effort to consolidate the institutions through which they could promote a fairer, more egalitarian world.

Ironically, in many ways, World War I resembled the events that marked the death of the old regime in prerevolutionary France—a pattern of developments which is synonymous with an old world dying and a new one struggling to be born.

Convinced that they had now outgrown their swaddling clothes, Independence movements among colonial peoples started to gather momentum even before World War II. In 1937, as a direct result of protest geared towards the alleviation of the economic, social and political plight of the working classes—the most direct victims of colonial exploitation, demanding better working conditions, better education, an end to poverty and hardship and an end to colonialism itself—the British Government appointed a Royal Commission under the chairmanship of Lord Moyne to investigate the causes of widespread rebellion in the British West Indies colonies.

The Commission's Report was a damning indictment on the administration of the colonies; finding fault with almost every aspect of British policy. Education, health care, housing, labour relations and economic matters generally were roundly condemned: *"The situation of the poor offers admirable opportunity for social reform,"* the Report concluded.

The Moyne Report also stated that claims for full representation were warranted to give the islanders a greater voice in their own affairs; pointing out that the growing political consciousness was sufficiently widespread to make it doubtful whether any reform, social or otherwise, would be completely successful unless accompanied by the greatest of constitutional development.

The movement of the 1930s had both a social and economic component; both of which aimed to break the embrace between the colonial Government and the landowning plantocracy. The vehicle for the transfer of power and influence was adult suffrage in 1951 that opened the doors to Lockean representative Government.

The march of history was firmly in favour of the masses; the prevailing model of society was "us", being the colonial class, and "them", being the new mass society ushered in by universal adult suffrage.

Independence fathers such as Alexander Bustamente, Jamaica; Uriah Butler, Trinidad & Tobago; Clement Payne, Barbados; T.A. Marryshaw, Grenada among others were foremost among those who threw down the gauntlet on behalf of the working classes in the watershed decade of the 1930s.

The political party in the Caribbean, like the trade union movement, emerged out of the struggles of the 1930s as colonial citizens, still fighting off the shackles of slavery abolished since 1834, sought to take the movement toward political and economic freedom one step further by targeting voting and labour rights for the working classes.

Ironically, the winning of adult suffrage and the political franchise was born of the need to create societies founded in freedom. As a corollary, political enfranchisement proceeded on the assumption that that would pave the way for economic enfranchisement and empowerment of the masses—the right and freedom of the masses to participate in society's wealth and property by redistribution: *social justice*.

This political movement, bearing the burden of its errors and successes, continues today, affected by the phenomena and forces that affect all movements and organizations that fight for the rights and welfare of the masses but which in many cases, like that of the trade union movement, have still not found the right path.

However, the postcolonial political party system *was* and *is* based on the premise that heavily centralized and top-heavy organization was the best means of challenging inherited colonial structures. This form of organization was predicated on one central concern—THE NEED TO ACQUIRE STATE POWER. Once State power had been acquired, the masses would benefit through popular policy initiatives.

This form of organization is, ironically, Marxist-Leninist; associated closely with the founder of the Communist Party in Russia, Vladimir Lenin. In a work entitled **What Is to Be Done?** Lenin sought to establish a method of organization which would lead the Russian workers to victory in the acquisition of State power.

He suggested that the Russian peasants were too backward, too unschooled in politics and the fledgling Russian workers' movement too fragile to be exposed to the naked brutality of the Tsarist State in Russia. Instead, Lenin advanced the theory of the Vanguard Party; a pyramid-like structure made up of professional revolutionaries at the top remote and distinct from the masses at the bottom.

Lenin's concept of the Vanguard Party, which was developed in response to conditions peculiar to Russia at the beginning of the 20th century after World War I, was taken by postcolonial leaders root and branch and transplanted into the Caribbean's postcolonial political ground without any attempt to contextualize or "Caribbeanize" it. That was the first mistake.

There has been much criticism of Lenin's model of the Vanguard Party. One of its most insightful critics has been Rosa Luxemburg, one of the leaders of the German Social Democratic Movement: *"The unconscious comes before the conscious. The logic of the historic process comes before the subjective logic of the human beings who participate in the historic process. The tendency is for the directing organs of the party to play a conservative role. Experience shows that every time the labour movement wins new terrain these organs work it to the utmost. They transform it at the same time into a kind of bastion, which holds up advance on a wider scale."*

The question now for us in St. Lucia, the OECS, and the wider Caribbean is: **How do we confront the challenges of the 21st century that began on January 1, 2001?**

The Trinidadian writer, C.L.R. James, advocated the complete abolition of Lenin's Vanguard Party model for the Caribbean: *"The theory of the Vanguard Party was a particular theory designed to suit a specific stage of development of society, and a specific stage of working class development. That stage of society is now past. The theory and practice that went with it are now an anachronism and, if persisted in, may lead to one form or another of counterrevolution."*

C.L.R. James was deliberately vague as to what should replace the Vanguard Party but suggested *"the complete and total mobilization of the popular forces"*, which he was later to describe as *"free creative activity"*.

The implication here would appear to be a constellation, a broad movement, a system more akin to *The New St. Lucia Model of Political Governance* as opposed to the narrow postcolonial, outdated Westminster model (see chapter 4).

CHAPTER 3

Late 20th-Century Crisis

The Social Contract
1762

JEAN JACQUES ROUSSEAU

Kings desire to be absolute, and men are always crying out to them from afar that the best means is to get themselves loved by their people. This is all very well and true enough in some respects. Unfortunately, it will always be derided at court. The power that comes of a people's love is no doubt the greatest; but it is precarious and conditional, and princes will never rest content with it. The best kings desire to be in a position to be wicked, if they so please, without forfeiting thereby their mastery. Political sermonizers may tell them, to their heart's content, that the people should be prosperous, numerous and formidable. Kings know this to be untrue. Their personal interest is that the people should be weak, wretched, and unable to resist them.

Archie Singham, in his well-known book on Gairy's Grenada in the 1950s entitled **The Hero and the Crowd in Colonial Polity**, wrote that Caribbean Governments have essentially been "personalist" forms of Government. A personalist form of Government is one in which the goals of Government, and even the aims of society, are predominantly influenced by one man, one person in whom power is concentrated.

Such a situation is not negated by the existence of competing political parties of relatively equal strength as these also depend on political personalization for their existence or winning elections.

Singham defined the relationship between these leaders and the electorate as that of a hero and a crowd. The personalist leader was a hero because he was able to elicit personal commitment from the masses to follow him. He used charisma, a quality the hero must possess, to mesmerize and propagandize the masses. The masses therefore participated only as a crowd in the politics of the country instead of members of a genuine political movement.

Some effort at providing a definition of charismatic leadership has been attempted. The German sociologist, Max Weber, in **The Theory of Social and Economic Organization** (Illinois Free Press (1947)), argued that the leader must have a calling and a self-confidence to initiate the charismatic claim.

Weber believed that the followers of the charismatic leader must have a package of unfulfilled demands generated by contradictions or limitations within the society that predisposes them to a leader who is believed to offer some hope of a solution. He believed it is when nagging hopes and confused selfhoods are defined with forceful clarity and precision by the emerging leader that charismatic leadership blossoms.

Weber defined charisma as a mystical quality of individual personality by virtue of which he is set apart from ordinary men and generally treated as endowed with exceptional powers or qualities measured in terms of the extent to which magical elements of thought are displaced by coherent, consistent thinking.

Indeed, it is difficult not to notice the repercussions of some of the power trips of postcolonial political leaders. Grenada's Eric Gairy openly posited that he was imbued with a "mission from God"; while Guyana's Forbes Burnham glibly talked about his "sacred dream" of a socialist Kingdom. St. Lucia's John Compton was famously known to "communicate with God in a helicopter" to decide the date of General Elections; whilst Kenny Anthony resorted to describing one of his fiercest critics, the late George Odlum, as "the great Satan" and promising "Armageddon" come General Elections.

More serious, if Massa was the instigator of psychological dependence in the colonial era, then our postcolonial neo-Massa politicians are now manipulating the dependency syndrome as they emerge into all-powerful and autocratic leaders who usurp the political party and make it their private fiefdom and becoming in the process third-world masters, kings, emperors and czars.

Those of us who are courageous enough to identify our own neo-Massa cannot have failed to realize the complicity of the people in abetting the whims, fancies, excesses, aberrations and extravagances of neo-Massa.

The eminent Russian poet, Yevgeny Yevtushenko, recently said of the now defunct Soviet authoritarian system of Government: *"Let's be honest and admit that it was not only the ruling clique that was guilty; but the people as well who allowed the clique to do whatever it wanted. Permitting crimes is a form of participating in them. And historically we are used to permitting them."*

Knowing of little else, experiencing nothing else, there is an all-pervasive antidemocratic trend in the entire Caribbean that is spreading from microcosm to macrocosm. It is gradual and insidious and more dangerous than seems evident; flowing from a tendency of overcentralization and a lack of faith in the power of the people to participate in important decisions of the State. In fact, what we see almost daily is an aberration of representative Government, a form of Government by tribalism in which chieftains rule by granting favours to partisans— with little or no contribution on their part; no self-reliance, no creativity, no courage to even consider alternatives.

There is a crisis of immense proportions that has revealed major fault lines in the politics of St. Lucia, the OECS and the entire postcolonial Caribbean. The postcolonial political party structure in the Caribbean faces immense pressure; it enjoys little esteem, faces widespread lack of interest, and not a little contempt. It is almost impossible today to find a St. Lucian or regional political party that is the recipient of genuine popular mainstream support, as was once the case in the immediate afterglow of adult suffrage in the 1950s.

The postcolonial political party in St. Lucia, the OECS and the Caribbean is suffering from a profound crisis of popular confidence that has, in turn, created an ethos of disenchantment in the general electorate whose message seems to be *"Stop me before I vote again!"*

In the postcolonial epoch there has been a search on to find new models of development which might be applicable to the region; but sadly short-sightedly, there has never been any real attempt to connect *social justice* to economic vision, except perhaps, in the case of Cuba.

That was a major political blunder which did not immediately manifest itself; perhaps due to the brazen haste with which the postcolonial leadership was willing to accept its notional national independence by seizing the political apparatus of the State from the colonial powers; believing the primary requirement for change was to supplant the colonial Administration with a local Chief Minister, Premier or Prime Minister without contemplating fundamental changes in the system of economic, social and political organization left behind by the colonial masters.

What the Caribbean needed most of all in the immediate postcolonial era was an enlightened attempt to correct the many inequalities of its social, political and economic system after centuries of colonial exploitation and impoverishment. The battle should have been a crusade against the negativity and counterproductiveness of our colonially inherited pattern of ossified social differences (the growing gap between the rich and the poor, the "haves" and the "have-nots") which have only served to intensify the confrontation between the various class layers in our societies.

Above all, it should have been a crusade to generate fundamental changes aimed at placing the economic, political, social and cultural destiny of these islands firmly in the hands of *the people* of these islands.

The path of economic development which has been slavishly followed in the postcolonial Caribbean has been and continues to be capitalist modes of production and development; in particular, the Puerto Rican model of development, sometimes referred to as "industrialization by invitation" introduced into the Caribbean in the immediate postcolonial era by the late St. Lucian, Sir Arthur Lewis.

The Puerto Rican model involves the attraction of American firms to establish branches in Puerto Rico, which offers lower wages and "tax holidays", and which, as part of the U.S. customs' union, has open access to the American market. But Puerto Rico is now hopelessly bankrupt.

This policy *had been* relatively successful for Puerto Rico in that it had led to a high rate of investment, rapid industrial growth and an impressive increase in standard of living and *per capita* income. But unemployment remained high and there were still widespread poverty and social inequality. Moreover, social transformation might have been achieved in Puerto Rico by incorporating itself into the U.S. economy but the price has been a loss of national identity.

There is little evidence of the Puerto Rican model achieving for Caribbean countries anything remotely like what has been achieved in Puerto Rico. Yet we short-sightedly persist in flogging a dead horse; offering fiscal incentives and other concessions such as the extensive alienation of land, beach and even passport rights to induce foreign capitalist investors in industry and tourism to establish companies locally.

Such a development strategy has only caused unemployment, poverty and crime to spiral. It was perhaps this that prompted the free-thinking Errol Barrow in 1986, and only a few months before his untimely death, in an address to the Heads of Government Conference in Georgetown, Guyana to bemoan the fact that *"Puerto Rico has become a launching pad for the neocolonization of the region".*

The adoption of capitalist modes of production and development in the era of decolonization was largely due to over four hundred (400) years of Anglo-American domination of the region. To most of the postcolonial leaders (no doubt influenced in large measure by the monetarist *laissez-faire* capitalism of the 18ᵗʰ-century British economist, Adam Smith, whose **Wealth of Nations**, published in 1776, was adopted as Holy Writ by economic individualists of the 18ᵗʰ and 19ᵗʰ centuries); free-market capitalism was the best way of achieving social transformation; oblivious of the fact that that might not be the best way to rebuild a people after the ravages of four hundred (400) years of slavery and colonial exploitation.

Since capitalism is based on the principle that individuals should be free to do as they wish, the motive for economic activity is often self-interest and profit maximization. Thus Adam Smith argued: *"By pursuing his own interest, he [the individual] frequently promotes that of society more effectively than when he really intends to promote it."*

Our love for unbridled capitalism also perversely suggests that we might be in love with our chains in that we have been collaborating in reproducing societies which made servitude increasingly rewarding and palatable; as Herbert Marcus pointed out: *"What started as subjection by force soon became voluntary servitude."*

Moreover, the colonial State that predated independence was the creation of the colonial powers. The political, social, and economic organization was instituted in order to facilitate the extraction of human and economic resources from the colonies in aid of the economic development of the powers themselves at the expense of the colonies. And, according to an

African proverb: *"The master's tools cannot be used to destroy the master's house."* (In other words, we would need *different* tools to do the job.)

In the 1960s the "Plantation" or "New World" group of Caribbean intellectuals, which included Lloyd Best, George Beckford and Norman Girvan, held the view that the Caribbean was colonized in order to be exploited by Britain and Europe; that Caribbean mercantilism was set up in order to enrich Europe, and by extension, America; and that the development problems of the Caribbean are directly attributable to the nature of the relationship that the Caribbean shared and continues to share with Europe and America.

The colonial State was never concerned with the social transformation of the masses and therefore made little effort in the social policy areas such as education, housing, health, unemployment and the eradication of poverty. Indeed, a state of massive unemployment was crucial for the existence of capitalism, being capitalism's "industrial reserve army" as Karl Marx described it.

The dynamics of the capitalist system suggests that, in the absence of Government intervention, the economy is capable of settling down in equilibrium with a large proportion of the country's resources unemployed—which is a recipe for social instability and disaster.

By the late 1970s many people who had previously supported the adoption of free-market liberalism as the cure for the region's quest for development were beginning to have second thoughts as fault lines started appearing in the economics of the free market. The market system had failed to achieve the social transformation that was anticipated: illiteracy, unemployment, poverty and disease became plagues in these societies. There was a tendency for many to wonder whether some other economic system might do more to lift the masses from the mire of poverty, starvation and hardship.

The hope and pride that the Independence movement had managed to instill in the people were destroyed as talk of market failure gained wide acceptance. Political freedom had promised so much but delivered so little in the way of the social transformation of the masses.

Inequalities in income and wealth were still very great in absolute terms and there is no doubt that they generated widespread dissatisfaction and resentment and had a negative impact on economic growth rate. Gross Domestic Product (GDP) and *per capita* income did not have much of an impact in the minds of the masses, convinced as they were that the distribution of income and wealth was grossly inequitable.

(It is true, of course, that Gross Domestic Product (GDP), the Government's indicator of economic growth, does not measure social hardship or reveal the real disparity of income or its distribution.)

Gross inequalities in the distribution of income and wealth further eroded confidence in the region's political, social and economic institutions; in particular, the made-in-England Westminster system of Government came under increasing attack.

As far as the new contemporary thinkers were concerned, Fidel Castro was God, Cuba was Heaven and State Socialism—whereby the State takes over the "commanding heights" of the economy by assuming the major role in the development process and the responsibility for directing, mobilizing and creating economic and social development—the only way to Heaven.

In certain islands, most notably Grenada and Jamaica, the State assumed the premier role in fostering growth and economic development and the nationalization of industries became the main feature of "State Capitalism" or "Social Capitalism" and socialist modes of production supplanted capitalist modes of production.

Unfortunately, this quasi-socialist experiment was short-lived due to certain strategic and fundamental blunders. The independent State was expected to manage economic power with a competence and capability no less than that of the colonial State and was hard-pressed to live up to such unfair expectations. Furthermore, Caribbean social culture is such that managers and employees of State agencies fatally adopted an attitude dominated by rigid bureaucracy, arrogance and insensitivity towards members of the public, such as can be found in the public sector today. There was also an unacceptable degree of party politicization and patronage.

Technical incompetence, insensitivity and political interference bred distrust and even resentment on the part of the public toward State control; and consequently tragically eroded political support for Statist options. As Norman Girvan, one of the thinkers of the period, observed: *"In the concrete context of the Caribbean political culture, State activities have shown a marked tendency to be politicized and used by the governing party as an instrument of patronage and reward, corruption and the perpetuation of power."*

During the last two decades of the 20th century, the postwar economic system known as established liberalism was replaced by a globalizing neoliberalism that favours international speculative capital and minimizing the role of the State. This has transformed the planet with regard to the expansion of trade, the rapid movement of capital, technology, work, *social justice* and the quality of human life.

We live in a dynamic and productive global economy that is capable of meeting the needs of all of humanity. Yet, because of Lockean liberalism and, now, neoliberalism, the vast share of the global economy goes only to a few powerful nations and to only a few people within those nations.

The present unpropitious world situation is not helped but rather exacerbated by trade and investment regimes such as NAFTA, WTO, TPP, and by the austerity and structural-adjustment measures imposed on nations by international financial institutions such as the International Monetary Fund (IMF) and the World Bank.

These free-trade, investment and structural-adjustment regimes have justified their devastation of democracy and *social justice* by sacrificing people on the altar of neoliberalism.

Since the 1980s the major trend in political and economic thinking in St. Lucia, the OECS and the Caribbean has been dominated by neoliberalism. With the defeat of Michael Manley's socialist experimentation in Jamaica, Edward Seaga led the region, in particular, St. Lucia and every Member State of the OECS, in following the neoliberal economists of British Prime Minister Margaret Thatcher and U.S. President Ronald Reagan who demanded orthodox economic plans as a condition for World Bank loans.

The approach to public sector management has been the Nobel Prize economist, Milton Friedman's approach, also called "trickle down" economics for its philosophy of providing advantages for the few who control capital in the hope that this would bring about economic growth that would eventually "trickle down" and redound to the masses in the form of employment, and so on.

The formula has been a straightforwardly simple one: reduce the public sector, which would result in a smaller public service payroll: cut welfare programmes: provide incentives to the middle and entrepreneurial classes to invest in the creation of economic growth, wealth and employment: privatize State-controlled industries: dismantle labour legislation and regulation = a freed-up economic environment.

The argument goes that from this almost Adam Smith *laissez-faire* approach will be derived the benefits of sustained economic growth.

In St. Lucia and virtually all other countries where this neo-liberal regime has been applied it has brought nothing short of havoc on *social justice*; it has resulted in greater economic stability; but not so social stability. The neoliberal plan, by dismantling the State, social infrastructure, and employment stimulus policies, has caused unemployment simply to spiral out of control.

There has been a great social price: inequality, unemployment and poverty. Very few scraps have "trickled down" and the poor as a whole has become poorer and the wealthy wealthier.

The so-called wealth-creating sector—in its own typical enlightened self-interest and to ensure a greater chance of survival, not to mention profit maximization—has imposed tighter profit margins, lower manning levels, cost-reduction measures and a greater reliance on technology.

Neoliberal globalization is not based on fairness; it globalizes only some areas, such as trade, investment, technology and intellectual property rights; ignoring human rights (including labour, trade union and employment rights), *social justice* and the environment. It is also biased in that it gives priority to *growth* over *development* and thus promotes the social exclusion of vast majorities of people.

The core of the neoliberal ideology is that an entity as complex as a State is to be treated like a company. But it is palpably clear that in these "companies", wealth is being increasingly inequitably concentrated.

An interesting study on Human Development made in 1999 by the United Nations' Development Programme (UNDP) revealed that the difference between the poorest and richest countries was 3 to 1 in 1820, 11 to 1 in 1913, 35 to 1 in 1950, 44 to 1 in 1973, 72 to 1 in 1992 and 74 to 1 in 1997.

The gulf between the poorest and richest countries grew by fifty per cent (50%) during the first two decades of neoliberalism (1980-2000). Also, the world economy recorded rates considerably lower than those experienced in the two previous (Keynesian) decades (1960-1980).

Between 1960 and 1980, total production per person increased by eighty-three per cent (83%) on average, while for the neoliberal decades the average growth per person was less than thirty-three per cent (33%). Three quarters of the countries around the world experienced a drop in their growth rate *per capita* of at least five percentage points from the 1960-1980 period to the 1980-2000 period.

During its thirty-year rule, St. Lucia saw a gradual succumbing of the Compton administration to the social monster of free-trade liberalism; with the merchant interest, including foreign capitalists, closing ranks to fight for the protection of their perceived share of the national cake at the expense of the discontented masses. What this misguided policy has brought St. Lucia has been widespread social inequality, cancerous social decay, sky-high unemployment, sprawling poverty and spiralling crime.

THOMAS JEFFERSON

Merchants have no country. The mere spot they stand on does not constitute so strong an attachment as that from which they draw their gains.

It is against a record of horrendous unemployment in St. Lucia and the widening chasms of social division that history will define the essential failure of John Compton's management of political power for thirty (30) years; which was followed by the visionless former SLP Government; and now, the unlearned neophyte, Allen Chastanet of the UWP.

After thirty (30) years of John Compton in the saddle and failed Labour Party policies, St. Lucia is saddened by one of the highest levels of unemployment in this region. With over two thousand five hundred (2,500) children and young persons leaving school each year in an economy that is structurally incapable of creating five hundred (500) new jobs annually, there is at least the prospect of some twenty-five thousand (25,000) young persons joining the ranks of the unemployed in the last ten (10) years alone!

Most St. Lucian children and young persons leave school without the faintest hope of getting a job. It is the same situation in which the majority of our children and young persons have been placed, ten, twenty and thirty years ago; and in which they will live—powerless to escape. These are indeed the "lost generation", lost because of thirty years of neocolonial mismanagement, neglect and incompetence by visionless UWP and SLP administrations.

There are long-suffering, public-spirited St. Lucians who followed Compton's budget offerings from 1964 to 1994. The recurrent theme in those budget presentations was almost invariably haranguing the private sector to *"create jobs on the infrastructure that is being laid down"*. Of course, that plea, like a dialogue with the deaf, mostly fell on deaf business ears with the result that St. Lucia has one of the worst unemployment situations in the entire Caribbean.

St. Lucia is not alone in terms of high unemployment. In the entire OECS there is wanton unemployment because all these countries are plagued with fundamental weaknesses in their economies that encourage high levels of unemployment. Antigua & Barbuda is also similarly plagued even though they may claim to have achieved some kind of superficial full employment.

The global situation in which Caribbean States have found themselves today is very different from how it was during the early period of self-government when the old parties mushroomed. The capacity of the political party to perform the delivery function after it had seized State power and translate into reality the hopes, dreams and aspirations of the populace was much greater than now; especially given aid and preferential treatment from former colonial powers.

Today the situation is markedly different. The antisocial policies of globalization and trade liberalization are now making the State increasingly meaningless. Once the State becomes meaningless, the political party too becomes meaningless. The result is greater apathy and disillusionment on the part of the general electorate which has manifested itself through massive electoral defeats suffered by incumbent parties in relatively recent Caribbean elections; including the shock defeat of the SLP Government led by the visionless Kenny Anthony on June 6, 2016, after only one term in office in favour of an equally visionless and clueless Allen Chastanet; who, rather obtusely, touts himself as the next John Compton!

The crisis of the State that is plaguing the Caribbean today applies to all the postcolonial political parties irrespective of whether they are in Government or Opposition; they exist in a symbiotic, bipolar relationship. One could not experience a crisis of such historic proportions without embroiling the other. The problem is, in a word, *systemic*.

As Professor Carl Stone used to say before his untimely death, any change of Government would only produce a mere changing of the guard—not any meaningful *regime change*.

And the 18th-century French writer, François Voltaire, critical of the French Revolution: *"Plus ca change, plus c'est la meme chose"* (i.e., the more things change, the more they are the same).

Both governing and opposition parties in the Caribbean appear to have lost the capacity to explain, offer solutions and organize society. One expression of this has been a decline in support for the main parties and a corresponding rise in support for the new phenomenon of "third parties" in the region.

The third party emphasizes a shift from the charismatic leadership of the early period of self-government to "technocratic leadership" as the only means of facing the challenges of the State today.

But it is far from clear whether a movement from charismatic leadership to technocratic leadership is the answer to the crisis of the State today. Quite apart from the very obvious fact that virtually all the "new third parties" in the Caribbean are effectively breakaway factions or splinters of mainstream parties, therefore, fruit of the loom; there is the even more serious problem that the crisis is not a crisis of Government but a *CRISIS OF GOVERNANCE*.

In other words, it is not WHO governs a country; it is *HOW* it is governed.

The political party as presently structurally constituted has now become totally anachronistic, meaningless and redundant as a means or method of organizing Caribbean society in the 21st century; and that applies equally to all the parties of the old regime, governing, opposition or third parties. What is now needed is no less than to *reinvent* the political party system.

A change from charismatic leadership to technocratic leadership is simply not enough; it's only a drop in the ocean in terms of what is required. A change in leadership is not synonymous with a change in domestic politics and no-one should assume that it is. A change of leadership without a corresponding change in domestic politics is meaningless; as development, *real development*, is an internal process, not an external process.

Nowhere is that more glaring than in the election of Dr. Kenny D. Anthony, a supposedly technocratic leader, to the leadership of St. Lucia on May 23, 1997.

And, as they say, the rest is history.

St. Lucia is now saddled with the calamitous Allen Chastanet.

CHAPTER 4

The New St. Lucia Model of Political Governance

I t is now universally recognized that poverty is, by definition, multidimensional and therefore the fight against it must be multifaceted. Thus, the great Tanzanian humanist and leader, Julius Nyerere, in one of his prolific works of writing posited: *"The fight against poverty, ignorance and disease requires the fullest participation by the majority of the people and an able and honest Government backed by a strong political organization active in every village which acts like a two-way, all-weather road; along which the purposes, plans and problems of the Government travel to the people at the same time as the ideas, desires and misunderstandings of the people can travel direct to the Government."*

Sen, Amartya, in **The Standard of Living** (Cambridge University Press (1987)) in his work on famine, proffered the concept that the desire of man for self-actualization is as important a basic need as food, clothing and shelter. Self-actualization in this context means access to basic education, to primary health care, personal safety, to the supply of information necessary to make informed decisions and to participate in the running of society itself.

Further, in **Development as Freedom** (New York, USA (2000)) Sen defined development as freedom, that is to say, the freedom of the individual to live the life that he or she desires. Such conceptualizations prod us to conceive of poverty as the nonpossession of tangible as well as intangible things.

Thus, people are deemed to be poor not only for the lack of adequate food, clothing and shelter (the basic needs) but also because of personal and social circumstances that limit the range of choices they are free to make in the process of self-actualization.

Indeed it is this type of development that has been the hallmark of the United Nations' Development Programme (UNDP). For example, a recent UNDP Report says: *"The basic objective of human development is to enlarge the range of people's choices to make development more democratic and participatory. The choices should include access to income and employment opportunities, education and health, and a clean and safe physical environment. Each individual should also have the opportunity to participate fully in community decisions and to enjoy human, economic and political freedoms."*

The yardstick used by the UNDP is the human development index that they devised as an alternative to the traditional *per capita* GDP measuring a country's wealth. This yardstick reflects not only income but takes into account such variables as the level of literacy, infant-mortality rates and citizens' access to health care and education in deciding how "developed" a country really is.

Launching the report in Barbados recently, Fernando Gambado, as director of UNDP's regional bureau for Latin America and the Caribbean, said: *"The annual series of reports sought to lend a new perspective to development, even to redefine development. The concept of human development places people rather than income or industry at the centre of development."*

This conceptualization has also influenced the World Bank. In 1999, the World Bank described poverty as *"multidimensional, extending from low level of health and lack of education, to other nonmaterial dimensions of well-being, including gender gaps, insecurity, powerlessness and social exclusion".* **THE NEW CONSTITUTION MOVEMENT** espouses the philosophy that far greater emphasis now needs to be placed on a BASIC NEEDS and PARTICIPATORY approach to development in St. Lucia, the OECS and the wider Caribbean. This basic needs and participatory approach rests on the recognition of the importance of the full mobilization of the human resources that reside in our people and channelling these resources into the stimulation of economic growth and national development.

We must go back to the basics and put the people first with a "human resource", "people centred", or "basic needs" approach to economic development; as opposed to the neoclassical, neoliberal, economic-growth concept of the past—the growth of income and profits without ensuring broad-based distribution and participation.

If we are to survive the austere challenges of tomorrow, we must formulate something *different*, today. The quality of life of the people is the most dominant economic, social and political issue facing us in the 21st century. To cope with this challenge, we will have to make some fundamental, possibly *radical*, changes in the very governance of our countries. A whole new economic system is needed as the economic system of the colonial past still holds us in economic colonialism.

But we must not only change our economic policies; also the very way our countries are governed as well. Because revamping the political system is the sine qua non (or first step) towards addressing our economic and social problems. Our economic problems can NEVER be resolved unless sociopolitical problems are first dealt with; in particular, the need to mobilize the people, which is a prerequisite to any forward movement. THERE MUST BE A ROOT-AND-BRANCH REORGANIZATION IN THE GOVERNMENT AND THE GOVERNANCE OF ST. LUCIA, THE OECS AND THE CARIBBEAN.

We desperately need to look at our political system with a view to reforming it. We need to devise a new political system that will be relevant to our needs and aspirations. The made-in-London (Westminster) model has not worked well for us in St. Lucia and the rest of the Caribbean. Instead of uniting the people, it has divided and polarized them and been a major cause of alienation and antisocial behaviour for large sections of the population.

The time to square up to the challenge of political and constitutional reform in St. Lucia, the OECS and the Caribbean can no longer be postponed. It is now for the leading thinkers and social scientists, indeed, all concerned citizens, to size up a new model into the 21st century; mindful of the fact that those who in the past set themselves up as the disciples of change are, in very fundamental ways, an intricate part of the old problematic crisis of governance; not the solution. We must now avidly look *for* the Next Generation.

During the course of a "Hope Dialogue" of resource persons that took place in St. Lucia in 1994, one of the persons who presented papers was Dr. Neville Duncan, Senior Lecturer in Government and Politics at the University of the West Indies.

In a paper entitled "A PEOPLE'S AGENDA FOR ST. LUCIA: MAKING LIFE MORE PARTICIPATORY AND PRODUCTIVE", Dr. Duncan stated that there are many ways in which it could be shown, in the specificity of St. Lucia, a political agenda aimed towards strengthening democracy could be made. The most formal, he opined, was to examine the

Constitution and make recommendations that would enlarge the opportunities for wider and more intense participation. This, he said, is a necessary task.

Dr. Duncan argued that we must be determined to change and provide clear and consistent indications of our willingness to change. *"One approach is to start with a critical institutional area and build upon the changes induced to produce primary, secondary and tertiary changes in other institutions such that in a relatively short time span, the whole collective institutional frame would be leavened by years of change."*

The established political party organization in St. Lucia, he thought, appears to offer such a possibility. *"It could be suggested that organizing politically to bring about some rapid and forceful changes would prepare the way most effectively for a revamping of the political order."*

THE NEW CONSTITUTION MOVEMENT believes we should look around for options within the existing political system but if that system cannot respond adequately or at all we must look beyond it for a new philosophy based on a strategy of *repositioning* the political system to accommodate fuller participation and representation.

Policy formulation under the old political order is weak, bordering on pathetic. It remains heavily centralized, secretive, politicized and amateurish—a casualty of the British-inherited, postcolonial political system known as the Westminster model. We must, as a matter of priority, address many of the anomalies in the political system, which is obviously not faithful to our peculiar social reality in St. Lucia, the OECS and the Caribbean.

The democratic spirit must be allowed to flourish throughout the length and breadth of St. Lucia by means of the decentralization of social, political and economic power through popular participation and representation. In short, we must decentralize the political system beyond the superficiality of the first-past-the-post system.

We must categorically reject what Maurice Bishop once described as "two seconds" democracy. For crying out loud, why should anyone believe that merely by placing a mark on a piece of paper on a ballot every five years, their life chances are going to improve significantly or at all?

Democracy should not consist merely of a game of electoral roulette played out at five-year intervals. The challenge is whether we continue to let one man and his cabal, (called Cabinet), run our country; or develop structures which provide for the different levels of participation, democratic control, accountability and representation that the different areas of national activity demand.

True (Rousseauan) democracy is about the courageous decentralization of social, political and economic power.

RECOMMENDATION 1:
THE NEW ST. LUCIA MODEL

The New St. Lucia Model will replace the Westminster model as St. Lucia's model of political governance.

RECOMMENDATION 2:
A TWO-TIER GOVERNMENT

Under **The New St. Lucia Model**, there shall be a two-tier Government structure as follows:

1. A CENTRAL or ADMINISTRATIVE or MINI-FEDERAL GOVERNMENT with responsibility for Monetary Policy, Economic Policy, Home Affairs, Foreign Affairs, Tourism, Trade, Investment and Infrastructure.
2. A SOCIO-POLITICAL LOCAL GOVERNMENT with responsibility for the Social Ministries: Education, Health, Housing, Employment, Gender Affairs, Youth and Sports etc.; and LEGISLATION, including ordinary legislation, constitutional legislation and amendments, and integrity legislation to enforce morality in public life.

This would be, in effect, a classical minifederation. It was very common especially in the 18th and 19th centuries to protect isolated and alienated communities afflicted by poor human and other communications with the centre while more and more power gravitated toward that centre. These communities, not without good reasons, developed philosophies calling for weak central Governments, entrenchment of local community or state rights and a dispersal or devolution of power from the centre to local regions.

The USA, Switzerland, Australia and Canada are all cases in point. And size is no matter; the principle is equally applicable. The Federation of St. Christopher (St. Kitts) and Nevis provides a good example; the Local Government of Nevis is responsible for all social policy matters on Nevis while the Federal Government in St. Kitts is responsible for general economic matters and foreign policy.

In the highly centralized system of Government that currently exists in St. Lucia and the Caribbean, we often see Government systematically increasing its power at the expense of localized, decentralized administration; and ironically in the name of democracy and accountability. Yet it is far from clear that concentrating power in distant centralism is necessary, either in the interest of democracy or of effective Government.

According to **The New St. Lucia Model,** several of the functions of central Government would be performed at a lower level of administration. Clearly those functions would be more responsive to people's needs if they were performed and financed at a local or regional level.

This has traditionally been recognized in Great Britain where Education, Housing, Health, Transport, the Police and many other Social Services have long been part of Local Government.

However, the trend of fifteen (15) years of centralist Conservative Government in the 1980s and 1990s under Margaret Thatcher and John Major respectively was towards increasing the power of central Government at the expense of Local Government. The Local Government structure in Britain is far from perfect. Some Local Governments are cumbersome and inefficient. They suffer from low morale and have difficulty in recruiting high-quality staff. They are also susceptible to pressure from vested interests, especially the political parties and politicians. But many people believe that the solution is to reform the structure of Local Government and not for central Government to gather all local responsibilities to itself. Local Government itself needs to be more proactive in order to cater to the needs of the 21st century.

In 1979, the new SLP Government ill-advisedly discontinued what was traditionally known as Town and Village Council elections. Indeed, the majority of St. Lucians, especially the youth, have never experienced Local Government (or Town and Village Council) elections. There was a time when these elections served as a stepping stone for future national politicians; especially in Castries, Soufriere and Vieux Fort where candidates contested them on a political party basis just as they do in General Elections.

But like General Elections, and possibly any area of activity where politicians are involved, Local Government elections were blatantly divisive and destructive. There were many areas in St. Lucia where Local Government created bitter social laceration and polarization. We believe that the reinstitution of Local Government elections is important as it would be useful to have one person, a highly visible person, with a popular mandate to speak for particular local areas. Yet, party politics, especially given the level at which it was conducted in the past, is just about the last thing we need for Local Government within the context of **The New St. Lucia Model**.

RECOMMENDATION 3:
INDEPENDENT CANDIDATES

Therefore, in the vision of **The New St. Lucia Model** being proposed here, persons will be nominated on the basis of their track record of service in the particular communities and not on the basis of political party affiliation; such that we could draw on the talents, ideas, enthusiasm, knowledge and expertise of people who would never dream of coming anywhere near party politics; THEREBY ABOLISHING PARTY POLITICS IN LOCAL GOVERNMENT.

Naturally, whoever is elected will be a political figure. But once elected, the popular mandate will give him or her (titled Senator) the legitimacy and the independence to speak for the whole of the LOCAL community.

RECOMMENDATION 4:
AN ASSEMBLY OF CIVIL SOCIETY

But even given a popular mandate, the elected Senator will be but part of a complex social matrix involving Civil Society Organizations (CSOs) as part of a SOCIO-POLITICAL LOCAL GOVERNMENT ASSEMBLY—a concept that would take these CSOs out of their comfort zones and into the realm of a people's movement towards *social justice*, good governance, transparency, accountability and responsibility: "Civil Society" being defined here as all the social groups and networks that are *outside* of the apparatus of Government which refuse to play a mere social or economic role but also DEMANDING a political role as well: Youth Groups, Women's Groups, Employee and Employer Organizations, the Chamber of Commerce, Professional Organizations, Human Rights Organizations, Media Organizations, Church Organizations, Civil Service Organizations, Public Service Organizations, Consumer Organizations, Environmental Organizations,

Diaspora Organizations, the Cannabis Movement—indeed, the entire creative chaos of civic life in the country will be part of this all-inclusive NO-PARTY PARTICIPATORY GOVERNMENT.

NATIONAL UNITY (1)

This sociopolitical Local Government Assembly is especially necessary as a means of promoting national unity as a precursor to the attainment of *The New OECS Model of Political Unity* as adumbrated in chapter 5.

All for one, one for all, that is our motto, is it not?
d'Artagnan to Athos, Porthos, and Aramis,
The Three Musketeers

THE LOCAL GOVERNMENT ASSEMBLY

It is this social matrix that will be the LOCAL GOVERNMENT ASSEMBLY (LGA) whose overall objective will be, among other responsibilities, the improvement of the social, economic as well as the physical environment of the locality; and which will open up the democratic and policy-making process to a far broader constituency in society and create a SOCIAL CONTRACT, a consensus about such matters as Government policy, direction, local and national development.

There are many issues, such as the role of the State, crime, employment policies, educational reform, agrarian reform, land reform, marijuana reform, housing, gender equality, tourism, regional integration, the fight against corruption, the fight against drug trafficking, violence and AIDS among other social, political, economic and national issues which this sociopolitical Local Government Assembly will be required to examine critically and mobilize action for change. It is about fighting for equality and solidarity as positive values as well as for *social and economic justice*. It is about a new and OPEN Government where FREEDOM OF INFORMATION will exist.

The New St. Lucia Model is, of course, a radically new construct because it is not simply about passive consultation *after* a particular policy is formed but active involvement and participation *in the actual formulation and implementation* of the policy. It's about a society free of poverty and oppression, where democracy extends from the workplace to the centres of political and economic power; a peaceful society where there is *justice* and equality between the sexes. We want decent and sustainable jobs for all; we want our children and young persons to have the real possibility of living in a better society. To achieve these worthy objectives, <u>we should aim for nothing less than a more effective voice at the very heart of central Government.</u>

In order to solve the sociopolitical problems posed by the challenges of our time, a more demanding agenda has to be generated by strengthening our organizations and raising the level of cohesion of our actions in a renewed spirit of national unity.

RECOMMENDATION 5:
PUBLIC SERVICE STAFF ORDERS

In this regard, all enactments similar to Sections 4:14 and 4:16 of Staff Orders for the Public Service of St. Lucia will be repealed.

Section 4:14, under the rubric "Public Meetings", reads:

"No officer shall call a public meeting to consider any action of the Government or speak or otherwise actively take part in such meeting. This prohibition extends to appearing on the platform at a public meeting which is convened with the object of considering or discussing a matter which involves the Government or the actions of the Government."

Section 4:16, under the rubric "Engagement in Political Activities", reads: *"Officers are expressly forbidden from engaging in party political activity at any time such as: (a) holding office or taking active part in any political organization; (b) criticizing the policy of the Government or individual ministries; (c) writing letters to the press, publishing books or articles, circulating leaflets or pamphlets or participating in radio or television broadcasts on political matters; (d) canvassing in support of political parties or in any way publicly supporting or indicating support for any political party or candidate."*

This would take local and national politics onto a new and more dynamic plane. Responsible democratic Government is a dual political carriageway; resting on the extent to which an informed and enlightened citizenry is allowed to participate in governing itself.

If you want a just and equitable society, you need policies that do more than merely maintain the *status quo*. Politics, and certainly not our small-island politics, is not primarily about mere management; politics is about ends, vision, priorities and policy; not business as usual.

RECOMMENDATION 6:
INTEGRITY AUTHORITY

Moreover, these newly created Local Government Assemblies collectively will be the new MORAL AUTHORITY or MORAL CENTRE of the nation with power to formulate rules and regulations for upholding morality in public life as well as constitutional legislation and amendments.

In Dr. Neville Duncan's paper "A PEOPLE'S AGENDA FOR ST. LUCIA: MAKING LIFE MORE PARTICIPATORY AND PRODUCTIVE", the professor spoke of the need to increase the involvement of nongovernmental organizations (NGOs) in the process of development in all the social sectors of St. Lucia. He thought that an outstanding variety of success stories has demonstrated the importance of finding ways through a reformed system of governance to release the energies of people within communities: *"Where insufficient or inadequate groups exist, Government should bring the stakeholders together on a collaborative management basis.*

"The reason is compelling: development is an internal process. Here in St. Lucia, the impressive work, growth and maturity of the Mothers and Fathers' Union should be noted and further encouraged. The challenge, therefore, is to strengthen and expand the number of community-centred programmes like those already in existence. A further challenge is that this approach should rapidly become the norm for the delivery of most Government services, mindful of the optimum scale of such delivery."

Dr. Duncan also observed that hundreds of Caribbean NGOs in their different nature, structure, size and purpose (and the private sector) continue to demonstrate the value of getting as close as possible to the direct beneficiaries and of breaking the chain of dependence.

This new system of decentralization, or devolution, or localization of power would, for the first historic time, mean that decisions are taken closer to the people who will be affected by those decisions. For crying out loud, it would prevent Allen Chastanet's disastrous DSH project in Vieux Fort.

There is much that can be learned from differing developmental models, so that our objective must be to work cooperatively with other organizations—both public and private—to enhance existing expertise which can be utilized within our nation. Experience has demonstrated that more can be achieved by drawing upon the unique contributions of individual organizations and directly involving the people in activities and policies that affect their lives.

It is necessary to keep the machinery of Government under constant review and to make adjustments to its structure and operational methods if it is to provide the necessary dynamism for the onward thrust of progress.

The new politics must be determined to draw on the widest reservoir of committed talent. The new politics must be concerned to ensure that the machinery of Government is radically restructured to make it responsive to the needs of a rapidly changing society; and, indeed, to be the principal instrument for initiating such change.

We have a situation in St. Lucia, the OECS and the wider Caribbean where the people are completely apathetic to what takes place in Government. They believe that affairs of State are the prerogative of a privileged few and therefore are not in a position to determine what takes place in their country in the name of development with the result that the masses shoulder economic deprivations while a select few enjoy what economic benefits their nation has to offer. The people have no say in the policy-making or decision-making process of their country and are therefore not committed to progress.

RECOMMENDATION 7:
AN ELECTED SENATE

St. Lucia's seventeen (17) electoral constituencies will be mutated to eight (8) LOCAL GOVERNMENT REGIONS (LGRs) which will collectively form an ELECTED SENATE in which all legislative and constitutional powers of the State will be vested. The elected Senate will be the LOCAL GOVERNMENT.

For emphasis, therefore, the St. Lucia Parliament or House of Assembly, as we know it today, consisting of seventeen (17) dysfunctional constituencies will cease to exist and be replaced by the Heads of the newly created LGAs (the elected Senators) which will be nine (9) in number (2 for Region 8, Castries, due to population density).

RECOMMENDATION 8:
NO LIMITATION

There will be no limitation on the power of the ELECTED SENATE by the Executive branch of Government by means of a veto or otherwise. The ELECTED SENATE will be the COURT OF FINAL APPEAL in the political sense.

RECOMMENDATION 9:
EXECUTIVE AUTHORITY

The Executive authority of the State will continue to be vested in the Prime Minister and his/her Cabinet who will be but the agent of the elected Senate and will therefore remain in office at its pleasure in the exercise of the latter's constitutional jurisdiction.

RECOMMENDATION 10:
JUDICIAL AUTHORITY

The Judicial authority of the State will continue to be vested in the Eastern Caribbean Supreme Court and in such inferior courts as the elected Senate may from time to time ordain or establish. However, the judges, both of the Supreme and inferior courts, will hold office during good behaviour and not on Government contract.

RECOMMENDATION 11:
POWER SHARING

Thus there will be nine (9) individual LGAs that will share power with the elected Senators at the local level; and the elected Senate made up of the nine (9) elected Senators that will share power with the Executive Prime Minister and Cabinet at the national level.

RECOMMENDATION 12:
AUTONOMY BETWEEN EXECUTIVE AND LEGISLATURE

The relationship between the Executive and the Legislature will change to give the elected Senate total and complete autonomy and independence from the Executive.

RECOMMENDATION 13:
INDEPENDENCE OF THE JUDICIARY

The relationship between the Executive and the Judiciary will change to give the Judiciary total and complete independence from the Executive and the elected Senate.

We should no longer accept the taken-for-granted world but rather understand a given situation with the persons in it within the context of the prevailing social environment. Social action should be based on previous trial and error.

RECOMMENDATION 14:
CABINET REFORM

One major problem we have inherited from Westminster is the assumption that elected representatives can also double up as competent Ministers. This can work in such like the British House of Commons where more than adequate choice can be made from a wide field to find good management material. But in the absence of such choice in a small House of Assembly of seventeen (17) MPs, as exists in St. Lucia for example, these two tasks should and will be separated; particularly in light of our history in being unable to produce enough competent people who can ably do both.

Government departments will be headed by trained technocrats and not by useless party hacks whose only claim to fame might be the ability to win a seat. Thus we would be able to draw on a wider reserve of committed national talent to head Government departments into the challenging tasks of the 21st century.

Ministers will be selected from professionals in the community. These persons will be managers, technocrats chosen for their expertise in a specific field. Certainly, in that choice there will be political influence, but the intention is to provide the country with high-level technical competency in Cabinet. As Thomas Jefferson once said: *our aim must be no less than the attainment of a truer and truer aristocracy*—Government by the best citizens; it is a case of competency versus party loyalty.

The Cabinet of Ministers will be nominated by the elected Prime Minister out of nonelected professionals in the community with a worthy track record in their particular field of endeavour. The names of the nominees will be subject to confirmation by the elected Senate after Senate hearings.

NATIONAL UNITY (II)

This new reformed Cabinet system will virtually guarantee the creation of broader-based Governments of national unity. Indeed, this is the historic moment to take a bold political step and dip into the wider reserve of national talent to bring those capable citizens who may not wish to venture into the arena of party politics into the circle of national leadership in CABINET. This is particularly necessary at a time when we must promote national political unity as a precursor to *The New OECS Model of Political Unity* (see chapter 5).

RECOMMENDATION 15:
MAKING ST. LUCIA A REPUBLIC

The inevitable effect of these reforms will be to inexorably elevate St. Lucia to the constitutional status of a Republic. The Queen will no longer be the Head of State, through Her Representative, the Governor-General. As a corollary, the Office of the Governor-General will cease to exist. The elected Prime Minister will become the new Head of State. The Oath of Allegiance will be sworn to the people of the State and will be administered by the Chief Justice of the Eastern Caribbean Supreme Court.

RECOMMENDATION 16:
LEGISLATION

Under **The New St. Lucia Model** the source of legislation will no longer be the sole preserve of the Executive or Cabinet. Legislation could emanate either from Cabinet or any Local Government Assembly.

In either case, the following procedure will apply:

THE FIRST STAGE

The proposition will first be sent to the Senate as a Bill for the consideration of the Senators in its committee stage. If necessary it is debated and may be amended. The proposer of the legislation is given the opportunity to defend the Bill. At this stage a filtering procedure will apply as a safety net against unmeritorious propositions.

Only persons who are serious, who have the right focus, who remain industrious, who seek out opportunities, are the ones who will succeed.

THE SECOND STAGE

Senators will now take the Bill down to his/her LGA for debating and voting.

THE THIRD STAGE

The vote will be sealed and signed by each Senator and taken back to the Senate for a vote. Senators will be imbued with persuasive authority but the constitutional principle of collective responsibility will be attached and applied to each Senator in respect of the voting decision of his or her Local Government Assembly.

Ordinary legislation will be passed by a simple majority but constitutional legislation and amendments by a two-thirds majority in the Senate.

A BOARD OF NATIONAL TRUSTEES

Under **The New St. Lucia Model** former Prime Ministers, former Ministers of Government and former Parliamentarians will be invited to serve on a board of national trustees.

NATIONAL UNITY (III)

Again, this is the historic moment for us to take a bold political step and dip into the wider reserve of national talent to bring others who have served their country into the wider circle of national leadership. It is particularly necessary at a time when we must promote national political unity as a precursor to *The New OECS Model of Political Unity* (see chapter 5).

RECOMMENDATION 17:
CIVIL SERVICE REFORM

The Civil Service will have to be accordingly reformed, restructured, redeployed and decentralized.

Each Local Government Assembly will have an administrative secretariat and the machinery to implement local policy decisions. The paid officials of the Local Government Assembly will be appointed by the Local Government Assembly and will be its Civil Servants.

The staff will be organized into departments on a functional/collaborative basis and each department will be headed by a Chief Official. These Chief Officials will be key personnel and their position similar to that of the Senior Administrative Grade of Civil Servants in the central Government Departments.

However, unlike the Administrative Grade, who are usually appointed on the basis of their general educational background and administrative ability, the Chief Officials in the Local Government Department will be appointed on the basis of their expertise in particular fields. Thus, the person in charge of the Finance and Education Departments of a Local Government Assembly will be an accountant and an ex-teacher respectively.

RECOMMENDATION 18:
LOCAL GOVERNMENT FUNDING

The annual expenditure of Local Government will come mainly from revenue income. There will be three main sources of revenue income: central Government budgetary allocations, local property tax, and a miscellaneous group of activities which brings income such as rent, interests, loans and grants.

RECOMMENDATION 19:
NATIONAL ELECTION

Under **The New St. Lucia Model** there will be institutionalized a National Election for the election of a person to fill the Office of the Prime Minister <u>for a fixed term of five years</u>. The National Election will be different from General Elections as we know them today and the proposed Local Government Elections.

Each of the LGAs will have the right to hold a local primary to select one (1) candidate to participate in a national primary; provided that where there is not more than one (1) candidate a local primary will not be necessary. Out of this national primary, the winner will have the right to contest the National Election against the incumbent Prime Minister; provided that a national primary will not become necessary in the event that there is not more than one (1) candidate who is desirous of contesting the National Election.

These challenging candidates should have the power and the platform to forge an alternative social and economic plank for the future and spell out the choices clearly and starkly.

RECOMMENDATION 20:
DEPUTY PRIME MINISTER

The elected Senator who commands the majority support of his peers in the Senate will be the President of the Senate, Deputy Prime Minister and Leader of the Local Government. The position of Leader of the Opposition will be abolished.

Thus **The New St. Lucia Model** is somewhat akin to the American system whereby the Vice President is the *ex-officio* President of the Senate with a casting vote. But, of course, there are notable differences between the two systems. **The New St. Lucia Model** is a completely new, organic and distinct political philosophy and ideology. Apropos of Leader of the Opposition, to criticize without being prescriptive is to nag; and neocolonial Opposition parties have traditionally been only adept at nagging.

RECOMMENDATION 21:
DEATH OR INCAPACITY OF THE PRIME MINISTER

In the event of the death or incapacity of the Prime Minister, the Deputy Prime Minister will become the interim Prime Minister for a period not exceeding ninety (90) days within which time a fresh National Election will be held to elect a new Prime Minister. He/she will also act in his/her absence.

RECOMMENDATION 22:
TERM LIMITATION

No person will be eligible to serve as Prime Minister for more than two (2) consecutive terms.

Kill an admiral from time to time to encourage the others.
Voltaire, Candide

RECOMMENDATION 23:
LOCAL GOVERNMENT ELECTIONS

There will be Local Government Elections held every five (5) years in each of the LGAs; each to elect its own Senator.

TRANSITIONAL PERIOD

The New St. Lucia Model reforms proposed here will be institutionalized within ninety (90) days of the approval of it by the electorate in a General Election. The Senators will be selected from the elected MPs based on the highest proportion of votes received. The next following General Election will be held entirely in accordance with **The New St. Lucia Model**.

RECOMMENDATION 24:
INTEGRITY COMMISSION

Since the Senate will be the Moral, Legislative and Constitutional Authority of the State this will effectively dispense with the need for any "Integrity Commission".

RECOMMENDATION 25:
IMPEACHMENT AND RECALL

Since the power of the Prime Minister is derived from the Constitution, his/her tenure will be at the pleasure of the Senate acting within its constitutional jurisdiction which will have the power to impeach a Prime Minister on grounds of misconduct, corruption, criminality, immorality, inability or incompetence in office; utilizing the constitutional procedure set out in Recommendation 16; ditto Ministers and Senators. The impeachment and imprisonment of President Park Geun-Hye of South Korea is a case in point.

WHY A NEW CONSTITUTION?

The Constitution is an important part of our lives. It is not simply a piece of paper; a Constitution must undergo change; it must be dynamic—that's what gives it vitality. The intendment of a Constitution is not merely to circumscribe citizens' rights into some narrow and corruptible flesh of a code; but rather to embody a conception of the nature of politics, of the source of political power, and ultimately of the good of society.

> *What man has made, man can change.*
> **Frederick Moore Vinson**

Just because a Constitution has formed part of a State for decades or even centuries (witness the manifold amendments to the American Constitution over centuries), it by no means means that it incurred an obligation to remain tied to it forever. No obligation in perpetuity is acceptable to human justice.

> *God gives it to me. Beware those who would take it.*
> **Napoleon Bonaparte**

And just as the Westminster model determined the constitutional structure of political governance that seemed appropriate to our postcolonial, twentieth-century needs and aspirations; so we must now alter and shape the structures that will be most appropriate to our twenty-first-century needs and aspirations in St. Lucia, the OECS and the Caribbean.

If the cost of these reforms is the drastic curtailment of the powers of the politicos, the Executive and the Prime Minister in favour of the power of the people through the Local Government Assemblies in the districts, and then the elected Senate in the city, it is a price worth paying for our democracy.

It is a little hard for politicians to negotiate themselves out of an omnipotent and all-powerful job; but if they really had the interests of the people at heart this is what they really should be doing.

The new system is designed to take control of the democratic process out of the grim hands of political party bureaucrats and establish a modality for negotiation and debate involving a wide matrix of social groups and movements whose different conditions and different aims give vigour and variety to our national life.

Democracy does not exist in a hermetically sealed vacuum but it is a living organism that requires the catalyst of free expression and public debate to energize it and to infuse it with creativity; to make it an instrument for the implosion of the latent talents of the people in a spirit of national progress. What we have in St. Lucia, the OECS and the Caribbean is a kind of "managed democracy"; a perversion of democracy.

For too long our (Lockean) brand of parliamentary democracy and the decision-making process have been seen as suffering from a democratic deficit. **The New St. Lucia Model** will oversee the release of much democratic energy.

This type of mass politics will become the basis of organized politics as well as a major institution of growth in the challenging task of nation building that lies ahead in the 21st century for the succeeding generation. It will awaken a sense of social responsibility in the people and cure the grave problems of apathy and alienation; responsibility being the mortar that binds society together.

No doubt there will be teething problems thrown up by alternative systems such as espoused by **The New St. Lucia Model** but when substantial sections of the population are subdued by feelings of alienation from the political process **The New St. Lucia Model** certainly has the potential to move the consciousness of the masses from a state of alienation to a state of activism.

But not only will **The New St. Lucia Model** render redundant the made-in-London Westminster model but also the role of the traditional Member of Parliament (MP). The abolition of the MP would prevent the deep-seated social lacerations and divisions associated with the old-style party politics.

The Westminster model opens the way for the manipulation of electoral boundaries, dishonest floor crossing by miscreant MPs; and it has certainly institutionalized much voter apathy and alienation. If the objective is to inject life into our jaded political system, if the objective is to liven and spruce up our democracy, then **The New St. Lucia Model** is the way forward.

A few years before he became Prime Minister of Trinidad & Tobago, Basdeo Panday, while addressing a congress of the then Opposition St. Vincent Movement for National Unity, called for a revamping of the Westminster model of Government practised in the Caribbean as the first step towards addressing the region's economic problems.

Panday was of the opinion that the region's economic problems could not be resolved unless sociopolitical problems were first dealt with. He said that the mobilization of the people was a prerequisite to any forward movement: *"We therefore need to look at our political system with a view to reforming it. We need to devise a political system that is relevant to our needs. The Westminster model has not worked for us in the Caribbean. Instead of uniting our people, it has divided them and has been a major cause of alienation for large sections of our population."*

Democracy in itself is not a distinct political philosophy. It is simply a commitment to a political system. "Two Seconds" democracy, therefore, is an inadequate basis for a distinct political philosophy. Any political system that does not develop and encourage mass participation in decision-making in the information age is *ipso facto* inadequate.

The New St. Lucia Model *is* a distinct political philosophy of <u>participatory democracy</u> that represents a commitment to the idea that people should have some form of control and involvement in the institutions and decisions which affect their day-to-day lives. It is as much a matter of sentiment as of ideology, of theory as of action. It recognizes that power has become remote from ordinary people who typically play out their lives in small roles within large organizations and institutions run by a powerful few.

It recognizes that power should be more diffuse or spread out so that ordinary people could control the people and the institutions that now control them. It is a model of participatory democracy which stems from the belief of popular sovereignty; that is to say, power is organic to the people.

<u>The democratic process is supposed to ensure that decisions which are arrived at redound to the benefit of the greatest number and that there is some substantial support for actions and programmes embarked upon in the oft-abused name of the people.</u>

YOUTH PRIORITY

And **THE NEW CONSTITUTION MOVEMENT** will not apologize to demonstrate a definite priority in favour of the youth.

On January 15, 1941, President Franklin D. Roosevelt, a product of a wealthy capitalist family, speaking to an American Congress dominated by the principle of free-market capitalism, on the occasion of his inaugural address, did not apologize for stating: *"The basic things expected by our people of their political and economic system are simple. They are: Equality of opportunity for youth and others. Jobs for those who can work. Security for those who need it. The ending of special privilege for the few. The preservation of civil liberties for all. The enjoyment of the fruits of scientific progress for a wider and constantly rising standard of living."*

"Equality of opportunity for youth and others" was the first basic expected by the people of their political and economic system in the estimation of FDR. We must demonstrate priority in favour of our youth in the formulation of national policies; not only because the youth sector comprises the largest single building block of our population but also because the social sector of the youth is the most energetic and connected sector with the greatest potential to facilitate or frustrate any new national thrust such as that of **THE NEW CONSTITUTION MOVEMENT.**

The youth sector is more amenable to change and better able to carry it out. Moreover, the youth are the ones that have traditionally suffered most from economic, social and political exclusion.

There is little doubt that St. Lucia, the OECS and the Caribbean are now caught in the grip of a multidimensional crisis spawned by years of visionless misrule; a crisis that exacts an increasingly heavy toll on the spiritual and material life of the people; especially the youth. Socially, the crisis threatens the very fabric of our society/societies; eroding and undermining accepted moral and ethical standards of behaviour.

Far greater emphasis will have to be placed on the basic needs of the people and a participatory approach to development. The new strategy which is required will be valueless unless the socially excluded people, in particular, the youth, the unemployed and the poor, are placed at the centre of the development process, both as an end and as a means to an end; in some kind of power-sharing arrangement with the politicians so that for the first historic time the socially excluded will have a powerful voice at the very heart of central Government.

The socially excluded must be so empowered and given the freedom to speak out from their own perspectives as they are often their own best advocates—their experience often moving and powerful—rather than suffering the perpetual fate of always being spoken for by pious career politicians and civil servants.

Isn't it rather ironical that postcolonial Government, which was set up to counter social exclusion, started and proceeded by excluding the excluded?

In **The Pedagogy of the Oppressed** (1974), the eminent Brazilian educator, Paulo Freire observed: "*A Revolutionary leadership must practise co-intentional education. Teachers and students (leadership and people) co-intent on reality are both subjects not only in the task of unveiling that reality, and thereby coming to know it critically, but in the task of creating that knowledge. As they attain this knowledge of reality through common reflection and action they discover themselves as its permanent recreators. In this way, the presence of the oppressed in the struggle for their liberation will be what it should be: not pseudo-participation but committed involvement.*"

As a corollary, there is one great task that awaits the full and enlightened consideration of **THE NEW CONSTITUTION MOVEMENT**: it is the pedagogy (or education) of the people. It is in this serious sense that knowledge is power, and education is empowerment, both individual and national.

To quote Paulo Freire again in **The Pedagogy of the Oppressed**: "*Democracy and democratic education are founded in faith in men, on the belief that they not only can but should discuss the problems of their country, of their continent, of their world, their work, the problems of democracy itself. Education is an act of love, and thus an act of courage. It cannot fear the analysis of reality or, under pain of revealing itself as a farce, avoid creative discussion.*"

In his classic study of political parties, Michels (Collier Books, New York (1962)) argued that the leadership and the development of a democratic organization are usually at cross-purposes in the particular sense that "hero worship", "the ego needs of a leader", and the uncritical thrust towards "efficiency" tend to establish an antidemocratic gap between leadership and membership.

The Machiavellian doctrine of the preferability of fear to love maintains that this gap is necessary. In **The Prince** (Oxford University Press, New York (1952)) Machiavelli wrote: "*It is better for the prince to be feared than loved.*"

The Machiavellian doctrine is thought necessary for the purpose of organizational control. But if the objective is more than social control; if the objective is also to develop national pride, self-confidence, national belonging and participation, then the military Machiavellian style of leadership must give way to a more human management. After all, leadership is not just about command and control; leadership is also about a vision.

Since democracy is rule by the people and, in our system, not directly but through elected representatives, the people must tell their representatives, and those seeking to represent them, what they expect of their political and economic system so that the people can be the proud masters of their Government and not its patronized subjects.

Our changing reality demands a continuing national debate among the populace, with the object of finding solutions to our sociopolitical and economic problems; especially the underlying ideological framework between poverty, *social injustice* and crime in our midst through a constellation of ideas.

No longer should the politicians tell society what to do but society should now tell the politicians what to do. The youth, particularly, must be made to feel, however inarticulate they may be, that their Government is now prepared to listen to them. They are tired of always carrying the blame for all of society's ills and problems when, in most cases, the young people are not the problem but have problems themselves which the Government has created for them either through its own actions, inactions or downright incompetence.

It is time the Government opened up a dialogue with the young people in a dispensation of Government where the political preachers are not damned liars and the resources of the country can be directed toward the greater welfare of the people in a renewed spirit that connects *social justice* to economic vision.

If the greater mass of ordinary people decide, own, risk and share then power will be more diffuse and the State less overbearing. We must recognize the role of Government, which is to regulate and steer but not to lead; Government needs to concentrate on serious long-term strategic thinking; that is the steering function. It is *the people* that must lead, they being the motor force of society, the engine. The parallelism with the car is an apt metaphor.

The basic philosophy of **THE NEW CONSTITUTION MOVEMENT** is that Civil-Society Organizations (CSOs) and Non-Governmental Organizations (NGOs) and Community-Based Organizations (CBOs) should be the basic force or engine that organizes society for the fight to transform living conditions (not political parties); and when the fight becomes a collective one it changes society itself.

But an engine can't run without fuel or maintenance. The same is true of CSOs and NGOs and CBOs. They are fuelled by ideas, a vision, motivation, boldness and a lot of guts and determination.

Slavery is not an acceptable method of organization. Only a free people and a free economy have the capacity to meet new challenges, create new activities and find new solutions. Politically, as well as economically, the role of Government is not to imprison but to unleash the power of the people; and in so doing create conditions for a society of self-confident citizens capable in time of achieving self-generated economic growth, progress and development.

Once society has developed the courage to give full play to the latent talents that reside in our people we will all be surprised by the contribution they can make to national development. This will not happen by creating and flaunting special forms of privilege and power but by allowing all the people the full freedom of the social, political and economic life of the country to which they belong.

The best Government is that which governs least: Local Authorities that create opportunities for people to get on with things. A society of free people is a richer society. Let people push down their own roots, establish their own stability and security; and society will be stronger.

But it is a vision of governance that can only be delivered by a new liberated and enlightened Government. It is not an approach which is open to neocolonial political parties, politicians and placemen; since, like the colonial Massa before them, our neo-Massa politicians fear the people and will never give them half a chance to prove themselves. They can never come to terms with this act of faith in the power of the people. They lack an enlightened vision of politics and political education.

The overriding need for political and constitutional reform and transformation, as much as any other issue, awaits the full and enlightened consideration of **THE NEW CONSTITUTION MOVEMENT**. It may well boil down to a choice between C.L.R. James' concept of "mass participation" (and empowerment), and the continuation of Dr. Eric Williams' concept of "Massa Day".

During his famous anticolonial speech in Woodford Square, Port-of-Spain on December 22, 1960, dubbed "MASSA DAY DONE", Dr. Williams described Massa as the white expatriate with a monopoly of political, economic and social power. But he also made the important observation that: *"Massa was generally white but not all whites were Massa. At the same time not all Massas were white . . . . Massa was determined not to educate his society. Massa was quite right. To educate is to emancipate."*

Massa Day implies the power domination of one group by another socially, politically or economically. Massa lives.

Despite the ostensible achievement of colonial independence Massa continues to stunt the development of both institutions and Constitutions here. Once we had hoped for the creation of democratic institutions and Constitutions through which a true Civil Society would flourish unshackled by personage and patronage, so we got rid of the colonial Massa.

But we were very naïve; we believed that the primary requirement for change was simply to replace the colonial white Governor with a black Premier or Prime Minister without necessarily looking down the barrel of the fundamental changes that were called for in the method of social, political and economic organization left behind by the former colonial masters. And now, colonialism has been but usurped by neocolonialism and the colonial masters usurped by the neo-Massa.

Neocolonial government and politics could never countenance the necessary process of structurally transforming politics according to progressive principles and values if politics is ever going to bring about significant and permanent improvements in the quality of the lives of the long-suffering masses.

Shut up and listen to your masters.
**UWP Government Minister, Clendon Mason; in response
to hecklers at a Political Meeting in Castries, 1979**

Massa Day is far from done in St. Lucia, the OECS and the wider Caribbean. The good doctor had also said: *"Massa is the symbol of a bygone age. Massa Day Done connotes a political awakening and Social Revolution."*

*When we win the by-election they will know who their masters
are in this country.*
**SLP Government Minister, Felix Finisterre; addressing
an SLP By-Election Rally in Castries, 2006**

Now is the time for the political awakening and Social Revolution that will throw out Massa once and for all and churn up what true political freedom and democracy is all about.

The fight for **freedom and justice** cost our ancestors and great-grandparents dearly. Many died. Many were taken away. Many went to prison. Sometimes they were defeated. But with each defeat grew the conviction that giving up was unthinkable; they had to go on to ultimate victory. They began to realize that a world that only offered poverty and hardship had to change.

It had to be ruled by the people themselves; because only they could protect themselves. That's why they called them "anarchists" and "brigands" and "communists" and "socialists" and "humanists" and even "nationalists".

They targeted the levers of power; some remained, some got lost, some gave up; but one thing was certain: they left us a better world than they inherited. We owe our children and our society nothing less.

There are fighters today as in the past because every generation produces its own heroes. But we lack the courage, conviction and defiance of other generations. We must replace our mindless, selfish materialism with selfless idealism.

We must summon up the cause of people's power, not necessarily to storm barricades but to impress upon our black and white neocolonial "Massas" the need for fresh thinking and for new voices to be heard. And if Massa respects history, Massa too will facilitate this exercise; for failure to do so will gradually transform patience into protest.

Freedom and Justice were never given freely; they had to be conquered. *Social justice* will never be given to us on a silver platter; we will have to fight to get it. And to get it Civil Society will have to stop being completely immobile and immobilized—we will have to take the CSOs and the NGOs and the CBOs out of their garages and fill them up with gas.

Raymond Williams was right when he wrote of the emergence of democracy as "the long revolution". For this "revolution" to be successful, established democratic participation and—to accept the full logic of democracy— democratic control and accountability must exist in all major areas of national life. This includes the economic, the social as well as the political.

And so, as we look towards the future of our country, we must see ourselves as part of a new Revolutionary movement; a movement to give power back to the people; a movement for popular participation; a movement for mass politics: **THE NEW CONSTITUTION MOVEMENT**. We must see our struggle as being closely related to liberation struggles around the world. Ours is a regional struggle; a black people's struggle for **Freedom and Justice**. Obviously, the anticolonial Revolution is not yet over!

CHAPTER 5

The New OECS Model of Political Unity

W hen the twentieth-century history of the Caribbean is written, the late 1950s will be seen as the era in which the Commonwealth Caribbean began to take its first tentative steps to liberate itself from the shackles of colonialism. In 1958 and 1959 respectively, two historic events took place: the Federation of the West Indies and the Cuban Revolution.

In 1958 hopes ran high that Federation would be the instrument through which the British Caribbean colonies (excluding Guyana and British Honduras, now Belize) would achieve some form of political and economic independence.

Since the early 1940s, Federation had been viewed as a means of enabling the small unviable British West Indian islands to group together for the purpose of achieving an independence which both the founding fathers of the Federation and the British Government thought they were incapable of achieving on their own as small-island nations scattered in the Atlantic Ocean.

The idea was being advanced that such a political arrangement would fructify and forge one single nation; economically strong, politically meaningful, and potentially great. It was even felt that a multiracial cosmopolitan West Indian nation might serve as a role model for a world dominated by xenophobic and nationalistic extremes.

Alas, the reality was less romantic; the rest, history: a combination of factors, including centuries-old interisland rivalries, inept federal leadership and the desire of the units to pursue competitive rather than complementary strategies for economic development conspired to bring about the demise of the Federation of the West Indies on May 31, 1962.

By the turn of 1967, three of the Federation's largest units—Jamaica, Trinidad & Tobago and Barbados (together with Guyana) had become politically independent and the smaller units comprising the Windward and Leeward Islands (now called the Organization of Eastern Caribbean States [OECS]) achieved full internal self-government through a constitutional mechanism called "Associated Statehood", with Britain maintaining responsibility for their external affairs and defence. By 1983, even the Windward and Leeward Islands had become separately politically independent, save Montserrat and Anguilla.

If in the 1940s and 1950s the case for the Federation of the West Indies was unanswerable, it is even more so today as the clouds of economic doubt continue to hover over more and more of the Caribbean Antilles—both Greater and Lesser—from mainlands to islands, from colonies to protectorates, even revolutionary frontiers such as Haiti and Cuba.

Internationally, the superpower cold war has been replaced by a state of unrelenting economic hostility between North and South; between developed powers and developing countries. With the death of the Soviet Union there has waged a great debate about the future of the South and whether it is at risk because of the unprecedented priority the West is giving to the East.

The East/South trade-off also ought to be viewed on another plane; the accelerated change in the economic balance of power. It is in the optimization of organization (the emergence of large regional groupings) that events in the East are likely to unfold; Eastern countries are being accommodated into a wider and more diverse European Union and NATO.

During the last thirty (30) years, a second wave of globalization has transformed the planet with regard to the expansion of free trade, the rapid movement of capital, technology, information technology, work etc. Today, all the industrialized countries belong to large regional economic groupings; such regional groupings as exist in the South are still tentative and ambivalent. Mexico was one of the first to understand the breakneck speed of developments and has integrated into NAFTA so as not to suffer from the extended EC market or the excessive redirection of European trade towards the East.

The East will no longer serve the South as a cold war channel for political bargaining with the West but a source of active rivalry and unforeseen economic change.

Developments in the international political economy have introduced new financial crises and have placed additional obstacles in the way of developing countries as they strive to provide more jobs and improve the standard of living of their people.

The Caribbean Community has certainly not escaped these convulsions. Increasingly, we are being left behind; marketing is becoming more and more demanding; technology is becoming more and more expensive and changing at bewildering speeds; capital is becoming more and more selective as to where it wishes to move; investment is no longer in search of low wage-freeze zones; and rescue packages from the World Bank and IMF arrive on our shores with strict conditionalities and the indignity of external supervision.

There is a growing realization in many developing countries that their economic future lies not in development aid from metropolitan countries but rather in the hands of the people of these countries themselves. In Africa, some countries, most notably Botswana, have followed these development policies since Independence. They tend now to be among the most prosperous and stable countries of that region.

Every indicator points to the need for urgent strategies which would move Caribbean countries onto a path of self-reliant and self-sustaining growth if we are to provide more jobs, more school places, better health facilities, more houses and a more diversified production structure and halt the steady decline in the standard of living and quality of life of the people. We cannot continue to tread the well-beaten path of our mendicant politicians and beg for aid and preferential treatment from former colonial powers. Our efforts must be redoubled and redirected toward internal restructuring and revitalization of our economies in ways that will utilize more fully and beneficially the indigenous human and physical resources of the region.

However poor we may be, however severe the economic difficulties we face, it must be clearly understood that the well-being and security of our people are our own responsibility. The so-called rich countries of the North do not owe us a living any more than we owe it to ourselves. In any event, no amount of foreign aid can ever produce the scale and efficiency of investment in productive activity on which our progress ultimately depends. **THE NEW CONSTITUTION MOVEMENT** believes that development aid and assistance, however welcome they may be, should never replace the need for people to grapple with their problems in a creative spirit of self-reliance.

Self-reliance in the context of CARIBBEAN INTEGRATION must necessarily mean collective self-reliance. We must strive through our own individual efforts as well as through regional cooperation not only to meet the present unpropitious economic circumstances but also to provide for the necessary long-term restructuring of our economies.

And it is at this juncture we must pause to think hard about the question of OECS and CARIBBEAN INTEGRATION in the 21st century.

In our present state of tension and anxiety, of trouble and turbulence, it is absolutely necessary to promote and defend the solidarity and sovereignty of the umbrella Caribbean Community. We must *reinvent* and rediscover strategies and mechanisms which will ultimately lead to unity of action in all major areas of our economic, social and political life.

July 4, 2018 marks forty-five (45) years since the signing in 1973 of the Treaty of Chaguaramas in Trinidad & Tobago.

But even as the "man in the street" vehemently swears by the gross failure of CARICOM, there must have been dreams, visions and aspirations of a Caribbean Community and Common Market blossoming into a viable economic and political force in the global political economy.

With the onset of CARICOM's Single Market and Economy (CSME), we need now more than ever before to examine CARICOM's unfulfilled promise. We need to ask ourselves: Why has CARICOM taken so long to deliver the promised land that the founding fathers intended that we should inherit; the CSME, a customs' union, fiscal harmony, industrial coordination, collective food security, a common currency?

Why has this would-be propulsion for the engine of our economic take-off and sustained growth failed to transform our economies into an involved state of self-reliance?

Over the many decades, CARICOM Heads of Government meetings have come to be seen by the people as little more than prime-ministerial talk shops; keeping us talking to each other until such time as we are brought together by the deterministic logic of history, the persuasions of social communion, the harsh realities of our notional national independence and by intellectual and political awakening to the point that we are the CARICOM that was foreseen by the deeper thinkers of the 1940s/50s.

Arguing the case for the federation of these islands in the 1940s, Norman Manley made a plea that has lost none of its brilliance: "*Here we are all on a sea of world conditions, stormy and hazardous in the extreme, each huddled on some little craft of our own. Some hardly have oars and only a few have accomplished a rudimentary sail to take them along. And here offered us is a boat, substantial, capable of being made sea-worthy and ready to be manned by our own captain and our own crew. If we won't leave our little craft and get into that larger vessel which is able to take us to the goal of our ambitions, then I say without hesitation that we are blind and purblind and history will condemn us."*

In view of our present unpropitious economic circumstances, the only question must be: How long, standing insularly, can we hold out in a storm in which developing countries are being tempestuously tossed about in the Atlantic?

Logically speaking, if there were an archipelagic area that could easily lend itself to a federal system of Government, it would have been the archipelago of CARICOM. Not only are we bound together by physical and historical accident, but also by similar economic circumstance; which means that we have a common purpose, a common aim, a common destiny—or a common fate.

We have a common heritage, consanguinity, jurisprudence, constitution, politics, secondary education (Caribbean Examinations Council [CXC]); tertiary education (University of the West Indies [UWI]); sports (West Indies Cricket); broadcasting (Caribbean Broadcasting Union [CBU]) and Caribbean Media Corporation (CMC)—not forgetting CBC (Caribbean Broadcasting Corporation); air carriers—BWIA and Air Jamaica (now Caribbean Airlines)—not forgetting LIAT; musical art forms—calypso and reggae; security systems ([RSS]—the Regional Security System); the OECS common currency, central bank, shared embassies and Supreme Court; and last but not least, the Caribbean Court of Justice (CCJ).

The eminent Caribbean economist and integrationist, the late William Demas, expressed the view that West Indians are all too inclined to harp upon insular differences which only contribute to "our rich cultural heritage", rather than concentrate on the ties that bind us.

And Professor Gordon Lewis, in his masterpiece, **Growth of the Modern West Indies**, took the separatist apologists to task: *"They harp on our cosmopolitanism when we are eighty per cent Afro-Asian, they speak about our differences, our various identities when we are fairly homogeneous in terms of religion and language, they talk glibly of economic disparities when we are all poor, and our separation by sea when a sun jet* *can run through the entire West Indies archipelago in-between successive meals."*

To the precious common elements of our West Indian identity, physical separation has, fortunately, offered no barrier. The real barriers to trade, movement and civilized living— which still divide and stunt the growth of CARIBBEAN INTEGRATION—cannot be blamed on the fact of physical separation; they are our own creation and bane.

And it is no consolation to realize that our man-made barriers are also an historical aberration: six hundred (600) years ago, a Carib or Arawak with a canoe boat could travel the Caribbean Sea— from Jamaica to Guyana—and transact whatever trade or barter he pleased—without passport, licence or quota. An indigenous native reincarnated today could never understand how we destroyed such a legacy.

If the myopic Caribbean leaders of our time have failed to grasp the essence of the CARIBBEAN INTEGRATION movement, the truth is: hundreds of thousands of ordinary Caribbean people do, in fact, live that reality in their mundane comings and goings on a daily basis. But it is to the bane and curse of us all that present-day Caribbean leadership is too lacking in vision and enlightened statesmanship to even begin to institutionalize a social, political and economic CARICOM that is more radical, more transformational and more inspirational than the tentative, half-hearted and half-baked CSME.

But any new thrust towards closer integration must come not just from a desire for social intercourse but primarily from a reasonable expectation, if not certainty, of economic advantage. In other words, not as an end in itself, but a means to an end— the social and economic empowerment and improvement of the life chances of the people.

Similarly, **THE NEW CONSTITUTION MOVEMENT** believes that the creation of the comatose CSME ought not myopically to be viewed as an end in itself but simply as the first tentative step towards a longer journey—the creation of a single political and economic space. The CSME is a crucial plank in any strategy to generate economic and social success for our people since our individual economies are almost certainly too small, open and fragile to provide the market base upon which substantial economic development must rest.

We must tackle the demand-side and the supply-side factors of our economies simultaneously for maximum growth; a regional trade base would facilitate the fruition of our goal of full employment by increasing the demand for goods and services.

The CSME, if anything, was too slow and tentative in coming; the economic cost of separation to everyone, from consumer to taxpayer, from businessman to Government, has been enormous. The fact is, hitherto the 13 Member States of CARICOM largely remained 13 separate markets ranging in size from 3,000 people in Montserrat to over 3,000,000 in Jamaica.

The movement towards a CSME whose citizens are free to exercise their vocational and professional skills and to sell their wares and skill sets from Jamaica to Guyana without seeking officialdom's leave would produce not only a regional division of labour but also create opportunities for transnational partnerships in a common destiny. Each of the 13 countries attempting to produce the same goods holds the totality of the region back by wasteful redundancy. Quibbling over the location of banana carton plants, flour mills, landing and fishing rights, the location of the CCJ and the incident involving the journalist Julian Rogers argues not against but for integration.

THE NEW CONSTITUTION MOVEMENT believes we must seek to create something of a centrally directed economic coordination and independence in which goods, services, people and capital can move freely without let or hindrance.

We believe that we should systematically and finally remove all physical, fiscal and technical barriers that divide CARICOM. To encourage trade flows and reduce high administrative costs, ultimately paid by the consumer, the physical barriers must be dismantled; technical barriers frustrate the creation of a common market for industrial goods which force manufacturers to focus too narrowly on their own national markets rather than on a regional trade base—with the concomitant increase in costs; fiscal barriers have also to be taken down if goods and services are to move as freely from one member State to another (as freely as between Trinidad and Tobago, for example, or in the case of the OECS, as between Antigua and Barbuda).

Unless we move towards a much lesser variation in tax rates and utility charges, we will continue to have unnecessary distortions in trade. Economic coordination and savings through greater efficiency would yield a tremendous cash incentive. But getting that coordination would be a task of a different order of magnitude.

But it would be wrong to look to CARIBBEAN INTEGRATION as a painless panacea; it would be at once a challenge and an opportunity; and we will all need to come to terms with its competitive cut and thrust to win our rightful place in an enlarged market. Any separatist adherents who may be tempted to opt out of the new dispensation would have grudgingly to watch it bestow increasing benefits to its participating members; and which would be denied them. And if they looked beyond the region, perhaps to NAFTA, they would see the challenge which, acting insularly outside of CARIBBEAN INTEGRATION, would overwhelm their relatively poor national economies.

Alone we can expect a marginal diminishing influence in world affairs, particularly Latin American affairs and both in trade and policy. As a strong and united CARICOM we can speak as a regional power. For example, it was CARICOM which was consulted by the Americans about the Haitian situation, not individual countries.

Ever widening cooperative efforts are called for now more than ever before; our problems no longer come singly but jointly: the Windward Islands' banana problems and the Leeward Islands' sugarcane problems are CARICOM's problems; ditto Dominica and the catastrophe of hurricane Maria!

There may be a tendency for some, particularly within the so-called More Developed Countries (MDCs), to eschew cooperative efforts and pursue instead insularism. In that *status quo* some may indeed survive but not prosper. Any national sovereignty which may be lost in CARIBBEAN INTEGRATION can be more than made up by a share in a much larger sovereignty. Ditto Aristotelian logic which holds that the whole is more than the sum total of its parts.

Some proposals to remove barriers will be greatly in favour of some countries; and others, which they may dislike, will be greatly in favour of other countries. But we cannot pick and choose; there can be no winners and losers; no "sharks and sardines".

Quite straightforwardly, the case for a new 21st-century attempt at CARIBBEAN INTEGRATION is unanswerable. In the words of then Prime Minister of St. Vincent and the Grenadines, James Mitchell (now Sir James), the Caribbean must unite *"for better, for poorer, in sickness and in health. Occasional one-night stands will not do."*

The case for CARIBBEAN INTEGRATION in the 21st century is, on every moral and practical consideration, the right one. It is based on the premise that deeper integration will bring greater economic strength that will benefit all Caribbean people. Unless we rouse ourselves, the inherent strength of CARICOM will remain idle and fragmented. We are wasting valuable time and opportunity by sharing too slowly and too reluctantly our regional resources.

Naturally, there will be problems to be surmounted in that kind of revolutionary process but only if there is political will. A decade of working together, and these problems would have been but a distant memory. However, every year that is lost in the absurdity of the existing situation exacts a terrible price.

Until we resolve to build a more coherent social, economic and political CARICOM, we will continue to place an unnecessary brake on the destiny of the region and the future of its people. A new form of federalism embracing a true CARIBBEAN INTEGRATION would mean such a release and increase of human energy and activity as to open up a whole new vista in the developmental history of the West Indies.

The vision which inspired and informed the founders of the failed Federation must be sustained because the prize is great.

But the "let's go it alone" option, even though plainly untenable, will always appear seductively easy by comparison. Like water, human nature always tends to take the path of least resistance.

The onset of the 21st century has brought with it a new era of change, challenge and opportunity. There is now renewed interest in the future of the regional integration movement, especially the need for the exploration of new initiatives and approaches to the promotion of economic and social development in the Caribbean. But the prophets of doom are hard at work—pointing to the federal failure of the past to forestall any progressive movement towards CARIBBEAN INTEGRATION in the new millennium.

It is at this juncture that we must pause for a whole new perspective look at the work of the now disbanded West Indian Commission (1992) and its Report whose "CALL TO ACTION" largely fell on deaf political ears and visionless political eyes.

The Commission was right! The time has definitely come for us to take a brave new introspective look at West Indian Federation in the 21st century.

In the 1980s, and towards the end of his political career, renowned Caribbean integrationist James Mitchell attempted bravely to put the issue back on the regional political agenda by making it a recurrent theme in his speeches. In what was described as a landmark speech in Tortola (May 27, 1988), Mitchell shook the West Indian world, perhaps out of its slumber by saying thus: *"By pooling our leadership resources at the political, technical and administrative levels, we will not only see the light at the end of the tunnel, we will escape the trap of the dead end we have got ourselves into. In my view there is nothing we are doing well by ourselves which we cannot do better together."*

In a "Green Paper" presented to the 1986 OECS Heads of Government Conference captioned "THOUGHTS ON EAST CARIBBEAN UNION", Mitchell chided his counterparts: *"All else failing, the region will virtually be stalemated in the stagnant backwaters of history. In that status quo, we the leaders will soon fade out or go under, one by one. We may even vanish with boredom from the scene. And the same fate, in the due process of time, is awaiting our successors facing escalating problems.*

"As I see it, we must have one flag, one anthem, and freedom of movement of people, goods, services and capital. Let's free up the Caribbean and move around like the Caribs and Arawaks did before the Europeans came to the region and carved it up in artificial segments."

Shuddering at the thought of entering the 21st century as a string band of meaningless mini-States, Mitchell called for a union of OECS States.

He considered time spent outside the business of unification as *"the wasted years"* and *"the era of idlers.... Delay is dangerous."*

As it turned out, the Leeward Islands, led by Vere Bird who thought it another attempt to whittle away at his hard-won "sovereignty" for Antigua & Barbuda, would have none of Mitchell's brainwave; whereupon the ambitious one set his sights on the closer-knit and homogeneous Windward Islands (Dominica, St. Lucia, St. Vincent & the Grenadines and Grenada): *"I know when two or three begin, others will follow."*

Sir James's idea of a political union of the OECS or even the consolation prize of the Windward Islands abysmally failed and marginalized into tedium, and not without good reason.

The idea never took any root outside the islands' ruling parties themselves. Indeed, the whole spectre seemed a highly academic exercise largely contaminated by politically self-serving interests.

And the fact that the OECS Secretariat found it necessary to edit Mitchell's "THOUGHTS ON EAST CARIBBEAN UNION", seen by many as an unabashed jobs-for-the-boys charter for the survival in office of the incumbents, did little to allay the fears of the people. Indeed, to many people the idea of union was born in Washington; what with the fact that the ruling incumbents were all members of U.S. President, Ronald Reagan's exclusive right-wing club, the Caribbean Democratic Union (CDU).

Neither the ruling parties nor their bureaucrats nor any combination of them made much mileage in the face of a sceptical people. They failed to prove to the ordinary "man in the street" how their refined meditations were supposed to impact on their mundane existence. And herein lies the acid test, the real test, the only test.

Their so-called Regional Constituent Assemblies (RCAs) held separately in each of the islands were a resounding failure.

The "deliberations" seemed a world apart from the day-to-day existence, dreams and aspirations of ordinary people. The RCAs could not as much as inspire the people to become participants in a debate in which they, for the most part, were relegated to passive television viewers; their destiny being decided for them through a process in which they had no real substantive input.

It is wrongly said that history repeats itself; it is people that repeat history. The first attempt at the Federation of the West Indies collapsed primarily because of the lack of the committed involvement of the people in that process as opposed to pseudo-participation.

The evidence suggests that none of the leaders of the Federation of the West Indies was seriously seized of the political intricacies and practical statesmanship attendant upon the establishment of a federation; they were always waiting for leadership from the Colonial Office in London instead of taking their lead directly from the people.

In fact, the British Government was often accused of forcing the West Indies to federate. In this sense, it was, in fact, a long-distance, arranged marriage, not a union based on love.

The federal negotiations were marked by a lamentable lack of popular input. There was not even the pretence of popular participation—although everything was professed to be done in the oft-abused name of "the people" by their "representatives" (as opposed to delegates) who spoke for them on the strength of their "mandate".

The representatives flew entirely at a tangent with the masses, travelling first-class to meet British officials in smoke-filled rooms and issuing press releases from VIP lounges of international airports. The result was a prefabricated federal Constitution rubber-stamped by colonial Legislatures.

From the inception to the termination of the federal process the people were marginalized and shunted to a side; their input not deemed necessary or important. They were not involved in the federal planning, its architecture or the construction of its structural foundations; nor when it was being taken apart piecemeal by insular nationalistic leaders screaming their heads off at each other in newspaper headlines.

In 1964, when an attempt was made to salvage the "Little Eight" (Barbados, together with what is now the OECS); it could not survive complaints by Opposition parties as to the secrecy with which that game was being played. Even the British Government Minister responsible for the colonies condemned it as a "veil of secrecy".

When the political tables had turned in five years, throwing up a set of "new" Governments, the new Governments themselves bypassed the people and rushed headlong into the "Grenada Declaration" in which yet another new grouping, this time including Guyana, was supposed to have been established.

And then, more recently, there was the so-called Manning Initiative that was born in some grand hotel in the Bahamas during the course of the 1993 CARICOM Heads of Government Conference when Trinidad & Tobago, Barbados and Guyana announced their intention to pursue CARIBBEAN INTEGRATION by themselves! The first time the people of these countries heard about the initiative was via television.

The matter of the form of CARIBBEAN INTEGRATION in the 21st century is of supreme importance. There are those who argue that the "F" word ought not to be used because of its negative connotations. During the course of the said discussions on OECS unity, Vincentian Dr. Ralph Gonsalves (now Prime Minister Gonsalves) suggested we should not be bogged downed by *"labels and definitional questions"*. However, history shows that it was that kind of definitional failure that dogged the 1950s/60s Federation.

The architect of OECS/Windward Islands unity, Sir James Mitchell, was in favour of a "unitary" as opposed to a federal system; with one central Government to direct both the economic and political life of the new entity and one central civil service and supporting bureaucracy—something of a United States of the OECS or the Windward Islands headed by a President.

This would mean, according to Sir James, among other things, the best political talent would "man the show" and there would be negligible attraction in municipal Government. Leaders would have to come upfront—no more back-seat driving as Norman Manley and Eric Williams had been accused of doing in the ill-fated Federation.

But the question remains, should these independent small States combine to create one single country—a unitary State with full sovereignty vested in a single Government?

What would be, then, the implications for the public administrations of these separate islands from the civil service to the police whose salaries vary from St. Lucia at the top to Grenada at the bottom?

It's easier to draw a blueprint for a superstate in theory than in practice. For example, the islands must choose between the single hierarchical structure of a unitary State with heads of departments and their secretariats located at the headquarters of the union; or a federal structure requiring a central administration but where officers will also be needed for the unit Governments within the federation.

In a unitary State, there must be uniform salaries; wages are significantly higher in St. Lucia than Grenada. There are also notable differences between their salary levels and those of Dominica and St. Vincent & the Grenadines. Any uniformity will have to involve the raising of emoluments to the level obtaining in St. Lucia.

The fact is a unitary State of the Windward Islands, the OECS or, by extension, the Caribbean, is simply not a viable proposition; it never was, and, never will be.

In the Mitchell-envisaged United States of the Windward Islands, for example, how would the new State be accountable to democracy? What would be the role of the people in the decision-making process? How would presidential candidate James Mitchell from *Bequia* in St. Vincent & the Grenadines address a public meeting in *Bouton*, a rural St. Lucian community where mostly French creole is spoken and understood?

It was certainly a dysfunctional element in the democratic process during the failed Federation that the heads of the two main rival political parties, Norman Manley of the West Indies Federal Labour Party and Alexander Bustamente of the Regional Democratic Labour Party, were both from the constituent island of Jamaica, which is physically situated some considerable distance away from the rest of the Caribbean;

physically cut away from the rest of the Caribbean by a vast expanse of the Caribbean Sea.

Those who advocate a unitary, centralized, United States of the region by this seem to mean nothing less than a fusion of all the islands of the Antilles, Greater and Lesser, sharks and sardines, presided over by a permanent congress. But this describes an annexation rather than a federation for the very obvious reason that relatively larger islands would dominate and overshadow the smaller ones.

The islands that are relatively economically weaker may themselves pay a terrible price if they enter into that kind of arrangement before their economies have become more developed; with a penalty of high unemployment and low investment as investors investing capital and paying wages in the same currency locate in the least inflation-prone, most productive and developed parts.

The freedom of movement implicit in such arrangements means that various elements—both desirable and undesirable— would easily gravitate towards the nerve centre as some islands become little more than glorified outposts.

Political organizations and alliances do not in themselves produce economic growth. It is not uncommon to see economic growth retarded by such political arrangements because hegemonies tend towards diseconomies. It was not for nothing that Jamaica and Trinidad & Tobago quickly repudiated the failed Federation of the West Indies.

The failed Federation was not helped by the fact that Jamaica, the largest unit with over half of the population and land mass of the entire Federation, was over one hundred and twenty (120) times the size of the smallest unit, Montserrat. In the allocation of the seats based on population, Jamaica was allocated 17, Trinidad & Tobago 10, Barbados 15 and each of the OECS 2, with the exception of Montserrat 1.

In 1958 ten (10) islands formed the West Indies Federation; by the early 1960s when bauxite had boosted the Jamaican economy, it opted out; followed by Trinidad & Tobago's Dr. Eric Williams (citing his famous metaphor: "1 from 10 leaves 0"). By 1962, it was "The Agony of the Eight", as Sir Arthur Lewis described it (Barbados and what is now the OECS).

In 1966, Barbados opted out in favour of its own political independence; leaving behind "The Lucky Seven" (the OECS) which itself disintegrated when Grenada became unfaithful by engaging in talks aimed at forming a union with Trinidad & Tobago.

CARIBBEAN INTEGRATION need not necessarily be confined to the present CARICOM but its vision should be broad enough to cover all countries washed by the Caribbean Sea, regardless of language or culture. The comatose Association of Caribbean States (ACS), which was supposed to bring together twenty-five (25) countries, including CARICOM States, five (5) Central American States, Cuba, the Dominican Republic and Haiti, was a step in the right direction in terms of the need to broaden our trade base.

But a genuine new form of federalism must transcend mere matters of trade; there is also the question of the disparity of economic power, for example, the huge trade imbalance between Venezuela and the OECS.

Deepening CARIBBEAN INTEGRATION must, of necessity, precede its widening, as the then chairman of the disbanded independent committee for OECS unity, St. Lucian, Hunter François (deceased), said in response to the formation of the ACS: *"If these small islands cannot get together and speak with one voice, they are defeating themselves. Before we spread out to people we hardly know (we don't even speak their language), before we embrace them in an association, I think we should get our own act together and speak with one voice. This is what is meant by OECS unity."*

Hunter François also expressed disappointment with the abandonment of the OECS unity initiative: *"We had so much public discussion and there was an undertaking that the matter should be brought to the Houses of Parliament. Up to now, this has not been done in St. Lucia. And now we are hearing of the ACS which is something wider and different and there is no explanation given as to why OECS unity has not been pursued."*

THE NEW CONSTITUTION MOVEMENT says **YES** to CARIBBEAN INTEGRATION but of a *radically different kind.* To counteract the tendency toward the development of a hybrid, foreign and alien superstate far removed and remote from the people, which was a major fault line running through the Federation of the West Indies, **THE NEW CONSTITUTION MOVEMENT** espouses that we must work actively towards the creation of *DECENTRALIZED FEDERAL STRUCTURES WHICH WILL BRING SUBSTANTIAL POWER CLOSER TO THE PEOPLE.*

The road to unity may not necessarily be easy. The destination, if the people of these countries so choose, would bring member States into a radically new federal association. The journey should preferably be slow and deliberate; it should be a process, not an event; it should evolve, and not be forced. It should not be a dramatic solution but a series of gradual steps.

Above all, in the new envisaged dispensation *THE PEOPLE MUST BE KING*. They must be involved right from the beginning of the decision-making process and not just at the end. We must let the people participate in every step of the way, at every turn, and in every corner; we must keep them informed at all levels and most importantly *WE MUST TAKE DIRECTIONS DIRECTLY FROM THEM THROUGH THE UNIT STATES' LOCAL GOVERNMENT ASSEMBLIES/ SENATES SITTING IN JOINT SESSIONS.*

The new strategy which is required is one in which the people are given a central and pivotal role in the decision-making process. It means that for the first historic time confidence must be reposed in the ability of the people to harness their own collective wisdom and channel this into the stimulation of economic growth and national/regional development.

This dilemma was well articulated in an essay by noted Jamaican and Caribbean economist and integrationist, the late Rex Nettleford, on the need to utilize the latent talents and the collective indigenous wisdom that hitherto lie idle in our human resources. Jamaica is the setting but it is the Caribbean as a whole he was addressing: *"The public opinion polls can tell you what are the feelings of a day or moment; they cannot tell you what are the deeper social and psychological needs of our people who have had to devise strategies and stratagems of survival against the ravages of severance and suffering and the continuing deprivation in economical, social and political terms. Such strategies are the result and clear sign of a collective intellect, a collective wisdom that resides among our ordinary folk. But that collective wisdom continues to be ignored on account of the arrogance of planners trained in the North Atlantic or even at the University of the West Indies, especially when the University forgets that it is not an extension of Oxbridge. The collective wisdom and intellect of our people are yet to be tapped and given central place in the development strategy of our nation [region]. But we are so busy Westminstering ourselves into becoming a clone of the Anglo-Saxon world and its American extension that we forget that we have a life and history of our own to be examined, dealt with and used as a source of energy for the development of this nation [region] and the shaping of a civilized society."*

But such a philosophy of development is foreign to present-day Caribbean leadership who would never countenance this act of faith in the inherent talent and creativity of the people.

The greatest impediment, therefore, to Caribbean unity has been the myopia and lack of enlightened statesmanship of contemporary Caribbean leadership. As a corollary, closer CARIBBEAN INTEGRATION is doomed for at least the expiration or removal from power of the present generation of Caribbean leaders.

The political philosophy that must guide the new CARIBBEAN INTEGRATION movement is one in which the people are given an effective role and function—one in which greater emphasis is placed on participatory governance. The failed Federation of the West Indies is there if only as evidence of the fact that any attempt at Caribbean unity is doomed if the people are not placed at the centre of the decision-making process. This must have been what Professor Gordon Smith had in mind when he, in his postmortem of the failed Federation of the West Indies, lamented the absence of "*a strong centre to act as a countervailing force against the fissiparous tendencies of the localist mentality*".

In **The Economics of Nationhood**, Dr. Eric Williams spotted a similar problem: "*Only a powerful and centrally directed economic co-ordination and interdependence can create the true foundation of a nation. Barbados will not unify with St. Kitts, or Trinidad with British Guyana, or Jamaica with Antigua. They will be knit together only through their allegiance to a central Government.*"

As far back as 1936, in an address to the Fabian Society (a socialist political society of the U.K. founded in 1884 that favours the adoption of socialism by gradual reform rather than by Revolution) Arthur Lewis (as he then was) expressed the view that as far as West Indian federation was concerned "*the real stumbling block has been the opposition of local potentates [leaders], fearful that their voices, all-powerful in a small island, will be unheard in a large federation*".

And Norman Manley referred to "*the vested interest of ambition in power, the most dangerous of all the vested interests*", as the greatest enemy of CARIBBEAN INTEGRATION.

In arguing the case for OECS unity both James Mitchell and Dr. Gonsalves saw the need for the proposed union to have a strong centre to hold it together—one central Government "WITH TEETH".

The rationalization of regional political parties may have to be a precursor to the new CARIBBEAN INTEGRATION; we may have to move from national to regional political parties. The obvious advantage is that regional parties will not simply be organic groups but will represent federations of political parties throughout the region.

The rationalization of political parties could also act as a catalyst for the realignment of the politics of the Caribbean in order to homogenize political philosophy and talent. In the failed Federation of the West Indies it was the West Indies Federal Labour Party and the Regional Democratic Labour Party which were the two teams projected on the federal playing field.

But given some of the disparities in size and economic power within CARICOM, a durable federation cannot simply be built by joining them together abruptly. Rather, it must be nurtured over a period of time in order to blend and bond; and it must be from the drawing together of relatively equal, self-determining but interdependent political communities. We live in an economically asymmetrical region. In some countries, there is strong industrial potential, while other countries are not industrialized. Further, this asymmetry is not only economic but also political.

Neoliberal globalization, intense competition and liberalization in national and international economic relations have produced considerable economic and social costs during the last three (3) decades. The rapid growth of the world trade in goods, services and finances have been accompanied by the growth of inequality within societies (both industrialized and developing ones). Inequality between the relatively poorer and richer countries in the Caribbean has been constantly on the increase, reaching unprecedented levels.

James Mitchell was right in at least one regard: *"If we continue to wait for the whole region to make the leap, then we are also expecting Venus and Mars to move in the same orbit. The process has to begin with a marriage of equals."*

We believe that the OECS should form the *first* concentric circle of CARIBBEAN INTEGRATION, followed possibly by Barbados, forming the second concentric circle. Ultimately, a form of CARIBBEAN INTEGRATION encompassing the rest of CARICOM would complete the integration cycle of an evolving regionalism.

During the failed OECS unity talks of the 1980s, William Demas recognized that the subregion may well carry the initial torch of West Indian nationhood.

The Organization of Eastern Caribbean States (OECS) came into being on June 18, 1981, when seven (7) Eastern

Caribbean countries signed a treaty agreeing to cooperate with each other and promote unity and solidarity among the member States. The treaty became known as the Treaty of Basseterre, in honour of the capital city of St. Kitts and Nevis where it was signed.

Following the collapse of the West Indies Federation, and prior to the signing of the Treaty of Basseterre, two caretaker bodies were created: the West Indies Associated States Council of Ministers (WISA) in 1966 and the Eastern Caribbean Common Market (ECCM) in 1968.

As the islands gained their political independence from Britain, it became evident that there was need for a more formal arrangement to assist with their development efforts: The OECS was established.

The WISA Secretariat became the Central Secretariat of the OECS and the ECCM, the Economic Affairs Secretariat.

In 1997, as a result of the restructuring of the Organization, the Economic Affairs Secretariat was merged into and became a Division of the OECS Secretariat (now the OECS Commission) based in Castries, St. Lucia.

The OECS is now a nine-member grouping comprising: Antigua and Barbuda, the Commonwealth of Dominica, Grenada, Montserrat, St. Kitts and Nevis, St. Lucia, and St. Vincent and the Grenadines; Anguilla and the British Virgin Islands are Associate members of the OECS.

AN OECS CONFEDERATION

What is proposed here is not a CENTRAL Government in the style of the failed Federation of the West Indies; but a *CENTRAL ADMINISTRATION*. Moreover, it is not a FEDERATION but a CONFEDERATION such as the confederation of thirteen (13) American States under Articles of Confederation (1781-89).

A NEW CONFEDERATE OECS GOVERNMENT

Each Confederate State would comprise of a three-tier Government structure as follows:

1. A CONFEDERATE OECS GOVERNMENT with responsibility for Monetary Policy, Economic Policy, Tourism, Foreign Affairs, Trade and Investment.

2. A CENTRAL or ADMINISTRATIVE or MINI-FEDERAL GOVERNMENT with responsibility for Monetary Policy, Economic Policy, Home Affairs, Foreign Affairs, Trade, Tourism and Infrastructure (but see below).
3. A SOCIO-POLITICAL LOCAL GOVERNMENT with responsibility for the Social Ministries: Education, Health, Housing, Employment, Gender Affairs, Youth and Sports etc.; and LEGISLATION, including ordinary legislation, constitutional and confederate legislation and amendments, and legislation to enforce morality in public life (same as in chapter 4).

The idea is to increase the countervailing power of small individual units in relation to the powerful external forces (including both Governments and companies) by forging a single centre of decision-making. Everything other than external contacts would be left to the individual units by giving them maximum autonomy and power of self-determination. This would avoid conflicts of sovereignty.

The OECS confederate Government would be headed by a President who would be a public servant elected by the Confederate States' Senates. The elected person would be called the President of the OECS and would nominate his/her Cabinet whose members must be confirmed by the Confederate States' Senates.

The Prime Minister would remain as the Head of the National Government as well as Head of State, according to the republican principles adumbrated in the preceding chapter.

The election of the OECS President should immediately precede the National Election for Prime Minister in the event that a National Prime Minister is elected as OECS President. Any citizen of a Confederate State would be eligible to be elected as OECS President.

Both the National Government and the OECS Government would be under the supreme direction of the people through the Senates of the Confederate States. Thus it would be the people who would determine the depth, breadth and scope of their regional integration process; and not the politicians.

The CENTRAL or ADMINISTRATIVE or MINI-FEDERAL GOVERNMENT with responsibility for Monetary Policy, Economic Policy, Home Affairs, Foreign Affairs, Trade, Tourism and Infrastructure referred to in (2) above would, in time, gradually be subsumed under the rubric of the Confederate OECS Government.

The result would be to altogether eliminate the second tier of Government and its Cabinet except for the Prime Minister who would be Head of State as well as Head of the National/ Local Government.

The EC founding principle of "subsidiarity" would be applied so that the confederate Government would only exercise those powers that cannot be more optimally carried out at local levels of administration. It virtually guarantees that governmental activities such as the provision of social services which are more responsive to basic human needs of people and accountable to democracy are performed and financed at a local level headed by the elected Prime Minister. Already, we've had a trial run. The OECS is to all intents and purposes a *quasi-confederation* of independent States that come together for specified purposes; although the Prime Ministers are supposed to act as "delegates" of their respective countries at their Heads of Government Conferences that make decisions which affect the entire OECS.

The only exception in the existing OECS arrangement is that individual countries surrender no sovereignty whatsoever and every one of them must agree to a collective will and do not have to abide by majority decisions. On the contrary, *The New OECS Model of Political Unity* does involve the surrender of such sovereignty as the elected Senates may decide to surrender to the OECS Confederate Government.

In the existing OECS model, since there is no political centre to enforce obedience, even unanimous decisions are usually flouted with impunity. It is in the institutionalization of a *radically* new political centre that *The New OECS Model of Political Unity* differs from the OECS model. For example, if the PEOPLE of the subregion voted to form a CONFEDERATION, under the Articles of Confederation, the Confederate States' LOCAL GOVERNMENT ASSEMBLIES/SENATES would be the COLLECTIVE WILL and the POLITICAL CENTRE WITH TEETH to make and enforce decisions. Again, not the politicians. The OECS Confederate Government would be but an agent of this collective will—with supranational powers whose instruments of implementation would not simply be declaratory but statutory.

The New OECS Model of Political Unity is clearly distinguishable from the "Cabinet System" that makes the various Heads of CARICOM responsible for different areas of CARICOM.

The New OECS Model of Political Unity and, by extension, CARIBBEAN INTEGRATION, is not simply about an alternative construct but an alternative society based on voluntary cooperation among people living and working in small, self-governing, sociopolitical communities—a virtual regional manifesto for action in the 21st century.

Index

C

K

Index

S

T

U

Printed in the United States
By Bookmasters